P9-CNC-451

Calming the Fearful Mind

CALMING THE FEARFUL MIND

Thich Nhat Hanh

Des Plaines Public Library
1501 Ellinwood Street
Des Plaines, IL 60016

PARALLAX PRESS

BERKELEY, CA

Parallax Press
P.O. Box 7355
Berkeley, California 94707
www.parallax.org

Parallax Press is the publishing division of Unified Buddhist
Church, Inc.

Copyright © 2005 by Unified Buddhist Church.
All Rights Reserved.
Printed in the United States of America on 50% recycled paper.
Distributed by Publishers Group West.

No part of this book may be reproduced in any form or by any
means, electronic or mechanical, including photocopying,
recording, or by any other information storage and retrieval sys-
tem or technologies now known or later developed, without
permission in writing from the publisher.

Edited by Rachel Neumann.
Cover and text design by Gopa & Ted 2, Inc.
Author photo by Nang Sao.

Library of Congress Cataloging-in-Publication Data

Nhât Hanh, Thích.
  Calming the fearful mind : a Zen response to terrorism /
Thich Nhat Hanh ; [edited by Rachel Neumann].
    p. cm.
  ISBN-13: 978-1-888375-51-0
  ISBN-10: 1-888375-51-5 (pbk.)
  1. Terrorism—Religious aspects—Buddhism. 2. Terrorism—
Religious aspects—Zen Buddhism. 3. Buddhism—Doctrines.
I. Neumann, Rachel. II. Title.
  BQ4570.T47N53 2005
  294.3'37—dc22
                                            2005015972

3 4 5 6 7 / 11 10 09 08 07

Contents

Recommendation

Promise me,
promise me this day,
promise me now,
while the sun is overhead
exactly at the zenith,
promise me:

Even as they
strike you down
with a mountain of hatred and violence;
even as they step on you and crush you
like a worm,
even as they dismember and disembowel you,
remember, brother,
remember:
man is not our enemy.

The only thing worthy of you is compassion—
invincible, limitless, unconditional.
Hatred will never let you face
the beast in man.

One day, when you face this beast alone,
with your courage intact, your eyes kind,
untroubled
(even as no one sees them),
out of your smile
will bloom a flower.
And those who love you
will behold you
across ten thousand worlds of birth and dying.

Alone again,
I will go on with bent head,
knowing that love has become eternal.
On the long, rough road,
the sun and the moon
will continue to shine.

—Thich Nhat Hanh, 1965

CHAPTER ONE

Uprooting Terrorism

O N NEW YEAR'S DAY, 2004, I arrived at the Los Angeles airport accompanied by 120 of my monastic students. I was asked to step into a small room to be searched. For an hour, security guards searched me and my luggage and read my personal letters. They also questioned a fellow monk, who had a Ph.D in chemistry, to find out if he had ever made bombs. The security guards were not looking for my Buddha nature; they were looking for my terrorist nature. We were in the U.S. to hold a retreat for people on transformation and healing, but they didn't want to know what good we could do. When a civilization comes to this level of fear, it is going in the wrong direction.

We have looked for strength and security in military might. We have attempted to defend ourselves with weapons of war. We have brought great suffering and destruction upon ourselves and others. Our way of dealing with terrorism is taking us down a dangerous path of distrust and fear. It is time to stop. Let us pause. It is time to seek true strength and true security. We cannot escape our interdependence with other people, with other nations in the world. Let us take this moment to look deeply and find a path of liberation. It is possible to look at each other again with the eyes of trust, comraderie, and love.

Understanding the Roots of Terrorism

We say we want to strike against terror, we want to destroy terrorism, but do we even know where to find it? Can we locate it with a radar? Can the army find terrorism using its night goggles and heat sensors?

Misunderstanding, fear, anger, and hatred are the roots of terrorism. They cannot be located by the military. Bombs and missiles cannot reach them, let alone destroy them, for terrorism lies in the hearts of human beings. To uproot terror, we need to begin by looking in our hearts. We don't need to destroy each other, either physically or psychologically. Only by calming our minds and looking deeply inside ourselves will we develop the insight to identify the roots of terrorism. With compassion and communication, terrorism can be uprooted and transformed into love.

If we look deeply, we can identify the real roots of terrorism. This isn't a superficial action. The roots of terrorism may be goodwill or religious faith. Some people commit acts of terrorism in the name of their values and beliefs. They may hold the idea that others are evil because they don't share these values. They feel justified in destroying their enemies in the name of God. People who engage in this violence may die with the conviction that they are dying for a righteous cause. And isn't our country acting out of the same conviction when we kill those we define as threats? Each side believes that it alone embodies goodness, while the other side embodies evil.

Fear is another root of violence and terrorism. We terrorize others so that they will have no chance to terrorize us. We want to kill before we are killed. Instead of bringing us peace and safety, this escalates violence. If we kill someone we call a terrorist, his son may become a terrorist. Throughout history, the more we kill, the more terrorists we create.

What would it take for us to be able to reach out to those who have terrorized us and say: "You must have suffered deeply. You must have a lot of hatred and anger toward us to have done such a thing to us. You have tried to destroy us and you've caused us so much suffering. What kind of thinking has led you to take such an action?"

I lived in Vietnam during the war there and I saw a lot of injustice. Many thousands of people were killed, including many of my friends and students. It made me very angry. One time I learned that the city of Ben Tre, a city of 30,000 people, was bombarded by American aircraft because some guerrillas had come to the city and tried to shoot down American planes. The guerrillas did not succeed and afterward they left. In retaliation, the U.S. bombed the entire city. The military officer responsible for this attack later declared that he had to destroy the city of Ben Tre in order to save it. I was very angry, but at that time I was already practicing Buddhism. I didn't say or do anything, because I knew that doing or saying things while I was angry would create a lot of destruction. I paid attention to just breathing in and out. I sat down by myself, closed my eyes, and I recognized my anger, embraced it, and looked deeply into the nature of my suffering. Then compassion arose in me.

Because I practiced looking deeply, I was able to understand the nature of the suffering in Vietnam. I saw that both Vietnamese and Americans suffered during the war. The young American men sent to Vietnam to kill and be killed suffered deeply, and their suffering continues today. Their families and both nations continue to suffer. I could see that the cause of our suffering in Vietnam was not the American soldiers. The cause was an unwise American policy based on misunderstanding and fear.

Hatred and anger left my heart. I was able to see that our real enemy is not man, is not another human being. Our real enemy is our ignorance, discrimination, fear, craving, and violence. I went to America to plead with the country to look deeply so that the government would revise its policies concerning Vietnam. I went out of love. I met with Secretary of Defense Robert MacNamara and I told him the truth about our suffering. He kept me with him for a long time, listening deeply to me, and I was very grateful for his quality of listening. Three months later, when the war intensified, he resigned from his post.

In the Buddhist tradition, we practice mindful breathing and mindful walking so that we can recognize, embrace, and transform our anger. Mindfulness can help us be aware of what is going on inside of us and around us. Anybody can be mindful. If you drink a cup of tea and you know that you are drinking a cup of tea, that is mindful drinking. When you breathe in and you are aware that you are breathing in, that is mindful breathing. When you take a step and you are aware you are making a step, that is mindful walking. The basic practice in meditation centers is generating mindfulness every moment of our daily life. When you are angry, you are aware that you are angry. When you already have the energy of mindfulness in you born from your daily practice, you have enough calm and insight to recognize, embrace, look deeply at, and understand your suffering.

Safety isn't an individual matter. Every one of us wants to feel safe and protected. No one wants to live in fear day and night.

Safety is a deep, basic wish of all people, of all nationalities. If the other people don't feel safe, then we do not feel safe either. If we threaten the safety of others, then we will feel threatened as well. It is the same with happiness. If your father is not happy and suffers deeply, there is no way you can be really happy. If your son suffers deeply, there is no way you can be truly happy. Thinking of the happiness of your son is thinking about your own happiness. The same is true with safety. When we consider how the others can feel safe, we feel safer ourselves.

America's Suffering

To succeed in uprooting terrorism, we need to first practice listening deeply to our own citizens. So many of us feel we are victims of discrimination, injustice, and exclusion. Poor people, the homeless, minorities, immigrants, those who are lesbian, gay, bisexual, or transgender, Jews, Muslims, the elderly, people with HIV/AIDS, and many others often feel excluded. America has not yet been able to listen to the suffering of her own people.

There is too much suffering already in this country. We busy ourselves doing as many things as possible, taking refuge in doing more and more, faster and faster. The more we do, the greater the suffering becomes. People suffer to such an extent that they can't bear to experience more suffering. We aren't sleeping well at night and we're not enjoying ourselves during the day. We can't focus on the suffering in other countries when we suffer so much ourselves; touching more suffering only overwhelms and paralyzes us.

We all have to suffer less in order to restore some kind of balance within ourselves. Only then can we engage in meaningful and effective efforts to build peace in the world. If we stop our constant activity and consumption, we can recognize that there is suffering inside us, born from ignorance, anger, and fear. We can practice breathing, walking, and slowing down in order to get relief. We can come home to ourselves as a country, recognizing and embracing our suffering. Practicing mindfulness, we see that our fear and anger are born inside our own country, not imported from outside. As a country, we can generate collective mindfulness to embrace our fear and anger. Together, with enough sensitivity, awakening, and insight, we can embrace our suffering. When we feel better, we get some insight, and we know what to do and what not to do in situations of conflict.

In a retreat for Hollywood entertainers in 2004, I shared that if directors, producers, and actors could allow the seed of happiness and peace in them to be watered, they could use their talent to make films that water the seeds of collective awakening and mindfulness. As an entertainer, you can help your country go home to herself, recognize her pain, anger, sorrow, and fear, and get some relief. This is the work of a bodhisattva.

We could use more films that focus on the suffering of this country. On the screen, people could see a person who embodies the suffering of the whole nation. The film would inspire the questions: Why are we suffering? What have we done that makes us suffer like this?

We suffer like this because in the past we have lived in this way, we have acted and said things in that way. Upon our understanding, the truth of healing will reveal itself. And then we will know what to do and what not to do, what to think and what not to think, what to say and what not to say in order not to make the situation worse, and to bring relief to ourselves and other people. In the process of the film, people could discover the truths about cessation of suffering, transformation, and healing. The seed of Buddha, the seed of awakening, the seed of love is in you. Despite what they sometimes believe, directors and actors aren't really concerned primarily with fame and wealth. The mind of love is very strong, and if they could touch this love, they would become bodhisattvas, and create films that lead people to awakening.

Helping Others, Helping Ourselves

When a doctor sees a sick person, she tries to identify and remove the sickness in the patient. The role of a doctor is not to kill her patient, but to cure the illness within him. It is the same with a person who has suffered so much and so has made someone else suffer; the solution is not to kill him but to try to help him out of his suffering. This is the guidance we receive from the Buddha, Jesus, Moses, and Mohammed. This is the wish of our spiritual teachers. It is the practice of understanding and love.

Perhaps someone close to you has been making you suffer through her speech and actions. Her speech is full of bitterness, misperceptions, condemnation, and blame. It may feel as if you are the only one who suffers. But the other person must have suffered deeply to speak and act in such a way.

You may be tempted to abandon or eliminate the other person. Sometimes a husband wants to kill his wife, to eliminate her so he can be free. But eliminating the other person is surrendering to your despair. What we need to eliminate is the cause of suffering. If you can help the other person remove the roots of suffering within her then she will no longer suffer and she will stop making you suffer. If you understand this, then you will try your best to help her not to suffer. So, helping the other person is helping yourself. This is true at both the interpersonal and international levels.

It is very important that we return to ourselves, and refrain from acting or saying things when we are not calm. It is possible for us to go back to ourselves and practice to rediscover our calmness, our tranquility, and our lucidity. There are ways that we can practice in order to understand the real causes of the suffering. This understanding will help us do what needs to be done, and will prevent us from doing what could be harmful to us and to other people.

After returning to ourselves, we can go to the other person and say, "My dear friend, I know that you have suffered a lot in the past. I'm sorry that I have not understood your suffering, and I have contributed to it by my way of reacting to what you have said and done. I don't want you to suffer and I don't want to destroy you. I really want you to be happy because I know that if you are happy, I'll have a chance to be happy also. I know that you have a lot of perceptions and ideas about me. You may think that I am terrible, that I am evil. I am sorry. Because I did not understand your suffering, I could not help you and I have made the situation worse. I am very sorry; I don't want this to continue. If you care to talk to me, if you care to tell me what is in your heart, what unskillful things I have done to you, then I promise I will do my best to help you and in the future I will refrain from doing and saying the things that can make you and me suffer."

This is the practice. If you are honest and you say it with all your heart, and if you are motivated by the desire to help, then the other person will open up and tell you what is in his heart.

Deep and Compassionate Listening

If the other person takes you up on your offer and begins to share, be prepared to practice deep, compassionate listening. Listen with all your mindfulness and concentration. Your sole desire is to give him or her a chance to speak out. Compassionate and deep listening means that the other person, or the other nation, has a chance to say what they have never had the opportunity or the courage to say, because no one ever listened deeply to them before.

At first, their speech may be full of condemnation, bitterness, and blame. If you can, continue to sit there calmly and listen. To listen in this way is to give them a chance to heal their suffering and misperceptions. If you interrupt, deny, or correct what they say, you will be unable to go in the direction of reconciliation. Deep listening allows the other person to speak even if what he says contains misperceptions and injustice. While listening deeply to the other person, not only do you recognize his wrong perceptions, but you also realize that you, too, have wrong perceptions about yourself and the other person. Later, when both of you are calm and the other person feels more trust and confidence in you, you can slowly and skillfully begin to correct their wrong perceptions. Using loving speech, you can point out how they have misunderstood you or the situation. By using loving speech, you can also help the other person understand your difficulties. You can help each other release those wrong perceptions, which are the cause of all anger, hatred, and violence.

The intention of deep listening and loving speech is to restore communication, because once communication is restored everything is possible, including peace and reconciliation. I have witnessed many couples practicing deep listening and loving speech to heal difficult or broken relationships. Many fathers and sons, mothers and daughters, and husbands and wives have brought peace and happiness back to their families through this practice. With the practice of deep, compassionate listening and loving speech, they have reconciled.

During a retreat in Oldenberg, Germany in the late nineties, after I gave instructions on deep listening and loving speech, four people left the lecture hall and immediately called their fathers. They practiced loving speech and listening deeply over the telephone. They had been estranged from their fathers for a long time, with no communication, and they knew they couldn't let this continue any longer. They didn't need to go back home in order to do the work of reconciliation. They just called their fathers right away. The next day they told us they had been able to reconcile with their fathers using deep listening and loving speech. Listening to someone with compassion can turn him into a friend. It may be that no one else has been able to listen to that person; perhaps you are the first one capable of listening to him and giving him the relief he needs. You become a bodhisattva, a being who ends suffering. You lose an enemy and win a friend.

A Council of Sages

America is suffering greatly. The destiny of a nation is too great to leave to politicians alone. We need people who can listen with their whole heart, who can listen as a human being and not just as a politician. We have to select those leaders who know how to listen, even if they are not well-known. I propose that the people of the United States form a Council of Sages who can listen deeply to people who feel they are victims of discrimination, exploitation, and social injustice. The Council of Sages could be made up of non-political people who have lived closely with suffering and understand suffering. They should also have experience in the practice of reconciliation and peacemaking.

We can learn from the experience of other countries such as South Africa where the Truth and Reconciliation Commission was established to heal the wounds of apartheid. The commission was headed by Bishop Desmond Tutu and received the support of both blacks and whites as a legitimate forum for understanding and reconciliation to occur. Televised sessions were organized where members of the different racial groups were able to listen to and be heard by each other, with the tangible result that blacks and whites could begin to find a way to coexist peacefully and respectfully in South Africa. This is a concrete example of the powerful effect that direct and compassionate communication can have on a national and international level.

The First Noble Truth in Buddhism is the recognition of suffering; the recognition of ill-being. The Buddha recommended that the first step in curing suffering be to understand the situation at its roots. The task of the Council of Sages would be to invite those who suffer in the country to come and speak out. The environment they create should be one of responsibility, of safety, and of listening deeply, because many people have great pain in their heart but don't dare to speak out. The practice will be a success if those who suffer are able to describe in detail their fear, anger, hatred, despair and hope.

I know that many public figures see the situation the same way I do, but they confess to me that they don't have enough courage to speak out. They are leaders in the political circle, in the business circle, or in the entertainment industry and they are afraid of losing their position. When I gave a talk at Riverside Church in New York, soon after September 11, 2001, my taxi driver was able to sit in the audience, although 1,500 people were turned away because there were not enough places in the church. The taxi driver, though not a political or business leader, shared with some of our monks and nuns that, "I completely agree with Thây's words but I do not have the courage to share it with the people around me."[1] It is not that the American people don't have the insight, it is simply that they don't always have the courage to speak it out.

It is not so easy for people to express what is in their hearts. To help them feel at ease, you have to practice loving speech, and encourage them with all your skillfulness and care. You have to create a safe environment, where they can be assured that they will not be punished or harassed when they speak their truth. The prac-

1   Thich Nhat Hanh's friends and students affectionately call him "Thây," a title that means "teacher" in Vietnamese.

tice of listening deeply to people who suffer inside the country can take many months, perhaps six months to one year. A Council of Sages could give people the space for this courage.

This is the basic practice of Buddhism, the First and Second Noble Truths the Buddha spoke of, acknowledging suffering and understanding its nature. If you don't understand suffering and the roots of suffering there is no way that you can understand how to get out of suffering. The Third Noble Truth is that suffering can be stopped. The Fourth is that there is a concrete path leading to well-being, the end of suffering. Understanding suffering is the prerequisite to ending it. In order to understand suffering you have to practice deep, compassionate listening. The Council of Sages will know how to listen with all their hearts and minds, without political motivation, focused only on understanding and relieving suffering.

The Council of Sages' sessions of deep listening could be televised so that the whole country could participate in this process. All of us have to learn about our suffering and the suffering of the people in our own country. This is a spiritual practice. Even though there may be a lot of technology involved, with microphones and television cameras, the occasion is very spiritual. You listen with no prejudices, only with compassion. The country may need to listen for many months until people can express everything that is in their hearts.

After the Council of Sages, along with the whole country, has listened deeply, we will know what to do and especially what not to do. We will have clear, concrete ways to stop the suffering, to give people a chance to smile and feel understood, to know that they will receive the support they need.

People have asked me, "What concrete steps can the American government take to reduce the suffering of the American people?" Representatives of diverse groups in the U.S. could answer this question in detail in the presence of the Council of Sages. Afterward, the Council of Sages could make proposals to the U.S. government offering insight into the current situation and concrete recommendations based on their collective wisdom.

Remember how much time the Senate and the House of Representatives spent discussing the sex scandal of former President Clinton? The Congress and the mass media wasted a lot of time, energy, and money discussing such a small issue. They made the whole world sick in the process. Yet the real suffering of people in America has been largely neglected. This is why we have to invest ourselves into this practice of listening to the suffering of our own people.

Since many of the sessions of the Council of Sages would be televised, the whole country could be involved in its own healing. Meditation is no longer the work of individuals; meditation in our time should be a collective practice. Many people think of meditation as a private activity, an individual sitting alone and contemplating "What is the sound of one hand clapping?" But the whole country can meditate together and look deeply at real questions of poverty, exclusion, and despair.

We have never really had a chance to listen to the suffering of our people, to truly understand their suffering. The practice of deep listening can bring a lot of relief, even before remedial actions are taken by the government.

The Most Beautiful Export

The second result will be that people around the world will become aware that America is listening to the suffering of her own people. This could inspire a lot of respect in other countries. This would be the most beautiful product America could export.

America has the potential to listen to the suffering of her own people and to remedy discrimination and injustice within. If you cannot listen to your own people, your fellow citizens, how can you listen to and understand the suffering of others? How can you understand the suffering in Afghanistan, Iraq, Israel, or Palestine?

Across the globe, people suffer from very much the same things: social injustice, discrimination, fear, and fanaticism. Fundamentalism is very much alive in countries around the world. Many people believe that they alone are on the side of God, and they behave as if they are the only children of God and the lives of others are not as precious. They want God to bless their own country above all, and not to bless others who they feel represent evil. But to think that everything the other group does is evil and everything we do is good, prevents us from understanding the values of others, and from recognizing their suffering and fear. Instead of making us stronger, our unwillingness to listen keeps us vulnerable and afraid.

God does not take sides. Jesus, Buddha, Allah—all the great beings speak of compassion and inclusiveness. We should not believe that we can be peaceful by eliminating the other side. Sessions of deep listening can help heal the wounds of fanaticism and this would be a wonderful gift for America to offer the world.

After taking the first step of removing discrimination, injustice, and inequality inside the country, America can then turn to those she believes to be the source of terrorism. I don't believe that the CIA, the Pentagon, or the Army can stop terrorism. It will take all of us, looking deeply into our human condition, to understand and help stop terrorism. A terrorist is a human being who needs help. Maybe the terrorist is you to some extent because you want to retaliate against those who have hurt you.

A doctor wants to destroy the malaria in a sick person, not destroy the patient himself. Terrorists are human beings who are sick with the virus of terrorism. The virus you see is made of fear, hatred, and violence. You can be a doctor for a person with this illness. Your medicine is the practice of restoring communication.

But if a doctor cannot talk to a patient, if the patient refuses to cooperate, then how can the doctor help? If the patient refuses the doctor's help, doesn't trust her, and fears the doctor may be trying to kill him, he will never cooperate. Even if the doctor is motivated by a great desire to help, she cannot do anything if the patient will not collaborate. So the first thing the doctor has to do is find ways to open communication. If you can talk to the patient, then there is hope. If the doctor can begin by acknowledging the patient's suffering, then mutual understanding can develop and collaboration can begin.

To resolve our current dilemma with terrorism we must be like this doctor. After our leaders have inspired confidence in Americans and proved that, as a country, we have the capacity to listen and understand, we can then turn to those who are considered to be terrorists. Our leaders can address them with loving speech,

"We know that you must have suffered and hated us very deeply to have attacked us. You must have thought that we want to destroy you as members of a religion, as a race, as a people. You must have believed that we embody evil, that we don't recognize your religion and your spiritual values. We are sorry that you suffer so much. We want to tell you that it is not our intention to destroy you as a people, as a race, or as members of a religion. It is not our intention to reject your spiritual values.

"We want to respect you. Because of a lack of understanding on our part, we have not been skillful at showing our respect, our care for you, and we have been caught in our own situation of suffering. Please tell us what is in your hearts. We want to understand your suffering. We want to know what mistakes we have made for you to hate us so much.

"We ourselves do not want to live in fear or to suffer and we do not want you to live in fear or to suffer either. We want you to live in peace, in safety, and in dignity because we know that none of us will have peace until all of us have peace. Let us create together an occasion for mutual listening and understanding, which can be the foundation for real reconciliation and peace."

The effort to understand terrorists must be made with the human heart. You can be a politician but you can be a humanist at the same time. Politicians need to be very honest when they talk to the people they think are the cause of their suffering. If America is sincere, if America invests all her heart and mind into the practice, then people will tell her of their suffering, and that suffering will ease.

If America can look deeply into herself and renew her great

tradition of freedom and tolerance, she will then be in the position to help other countries establish similar forums, to invite other groups and countries to express themselves as well.

If America is successful in creating a Council of Sages, an international Council of Sages could be formed to create a forum for listening to the difficulties and the real situations of groups and nations that are believed to be the base for terrorist activity. A safe and peaceful setting should be arranged for representatives of conflicting groups and nations to practice looking deeply. The information and insights gained from listening to the suffering of others will help them to understand the situation more clearly and make recommendations.

This practice should be conducted as a non-political activity, supervised by humanitarian and spiritual leaders who are known to be free from discrimination and partisanship. They don't need to be famous people. People who know how to sit quietly and listen with all their attention can be invited to come and create an atmosphere of peace and non-fear so that those who suffer will have the chance, the inspiration, and the desire to express what is in their hearts. We must be patient. The process of learning about each other's suffering will take time because the suffering is enormous.

Countries representing every continent should be invited to sponsor and support this practice. These countries can come together, not as enemies that bomb and destroy, but as wise people. People from different cultures and civilizations would have the opportunity to speak and listen to one another as brothers and sisters who inhabit the same planet.

Negotiations for peace, reconciliation, and mutual cooperation between conflicting peoples and nations could be made based on the insights gained from this process. People from each country could participate in each step of the process by expressing their insights and their support for a peaceful resolution. Military and political leaders could also participate in this process, primarily as listeners.

Priority to speak would be given to those whose voices are not already represented in the decision-making process, such as schoolteachers, spiritual leaders, doctors, parents, union and non-union workers, business people, artists, writers, children, social workers, experienced mediators, psychologists, and nurses.

If such an international forum were broadcast around the world, billions of people could practice the First and Second Noble Truths offered by the Buddha, the awareness of suffering and the awareness of the causes of suffering. Understanding suffering is the foundation of any good action, whether it is political, social, or spiritual. Two steps on the Buddha's Eight-Fold Path to ending suffering are Right Action and Right Understanding.[2] If Congress doesn't engage in Right Action it is because it doesn't have Right Understanding about the suffering within our own country and in the world. Understanding the suffering of your own people is the foundation of all beneficial political action. Education will be good education if it is based on right understanding of the suffering of adults

---

2   The Buddha described the Noble Eightfold Path as the way out of suffering. Its elements are: Right Understanding, Right Thoughts, Right Speech, Right Action, Right Livelihood, Right Effort, Right Mindfulness, and Right Concentration.

and children. Deep listening and loving speech are wonderful instruments to gain Right Understanding that can then be the foundation of your action.

Right Understanding involves understanding suffering and seeing what governments could do to make social justice, mutual respect, and tolerance a reality. If we need one, two, or three years, we must take this time to practice deep listening. We have waged wars that went on for ten, twenty, even one hundred years. Organizing a session of deep listening is the practice of peace. One or two years of this kind of reconciliation is not long, but it can bring great results: true and profound understanding of the suffering inside and around us.

This is engaged Buddhism. This is the kind of Buddhism that can be practiced in the political, social, and economic arena. This is the up-to-date application of the Four Noble Truths and the Eightfold Path leading to the cessation of suffering. It is not a theory; it is real life. In Plum Village and at retreats around the world, we have helped so many families and couples solve their problems using these methods.

A Peace Conference As a Retreat

Every summer, Plum Village, a meditation community in France, hosts a group of several dozen Palestinians and Israelis. At the beginning of each retreat, many of the participants are unable to look at each other or talk to each other. By the end of two weeks, they sit together as brothers and sisters. This is due to practicing mindfulness together, eating in mindfulness, walking together, listening deeply to each other, and using loving speech.

Because of our very positive experience with helping to facilitate reconciliation, it is my hope that countries can come together to organize a setting like Plum Village on a large scale. What are now called "peace talks" are meetings where people continue to fight each other with words of fear and anger. But we could organize a peace conference as a real retreat, sponsored by as many powerful countries and international organizations as possible. It would unfold in a calm atmosphere where participants can walk peacefully and look at each other with kind eyes. This will help people be inspired to share what is in their heart.

Our politicians have tried very hard to negotiate peace accords and agreements using the tools of discussion and debate. If we can create a setting where we use the tools of mindfulness, where people can learn to walk with awareness, to breathe, to practice total relaxation, and to embrace their fear and strong emotions, then there will be a chance for peace. If you do not know how to take care of your fear, anger, and despair, if you do not know how to calm yourself, how can you negotiate peace?

BELIEVING IN OUR SPIRITUAL PATH

Many of us claim to be disciples of the Buddha, of Jesus Christ, of Mohammed, but we don't listen to their teachings. Hatred cannot overcome hatred. Violence cannot overcome violence. The Bible, the Koran, the Torah, and the Sutras teach us that. But we don't always believe in our spiritual path. We must think that our spiritual teachings are not realistic, because we have put so much faith in military and financial power. We think that money and weapons can make us strong. But our country has a lot of weapons and a lot of money and we are still very afraid and insecure.

The only way we can protect ourselves is with understanding and compassion. Only when understanding and compassion embrace you and the other person does safety become a reality. Even after just one international session of listening, everyone would learn so much about the actual suffering in the world. Appropriate political and social solutions can only arise when suffering is acknowledged and understood. Only with understanding is healing possible. The Buddha is there and shows us the way.

In taking these steps to organize national and international sessions of listening, America would show great courage and spiritual strength and could make a great contribution to the peace and safety of the whole world. Acting in the spirit of Thomas Jefferson, Abraham Lincoln, and Martin Luther King, Jr., this country can promote democracy and mutual respect among peoples of different backgrounds and beliefs. With our greater understanding, we can help create peace and security for everyone.

CHAPTER TWO

Compassion Is Our Best Protection

THE REVELATION of the abuse of prisoners of war in Iraq, Afghanistan, and Guantanamo Bay, Cuba provides us with the opportunity to look deeply into the nature of war. This is an opportunity for us to be more aware, for these abuses reveal the truth about what actually goes on during war and conflict. This isn't new—everywhere that there is war, there is abuse and torture of prisoners.

Soldiers are trained to kill as many people as possible and as quickly as possible. Soldiers are told that if they don't kill, they will be killed. They're taught that killing is good because the people they are trying to kill are dangerous to society; that the *others* are demons and our nation would be better off without them. Soldiers are trained to believe they *must* kill the other group because these others aren't human beings. If soldiers see their "enemies" as human beings just like themselves, they would have no courage to kill them. Every one of us should be aware of how soldiers are trained, whether or not we think we agree with the fighting. It is important not to blame and single out any country. The situation is more a consequence of our way of fighting rather than something particular to the United States. During the Vietnam War, atrocities were committed by both sides.

When the torture was revealed, President Bush responded by

saying that the U.S. had sent dedicated young soldiers, not abusers, to Iraq. This statement showed a lack of understanding of war that shocked me because the torture and abuse these soldiers engaged in was the direct result of the training they had undergone. The training already makes them lose their humanity. The young men going to Iraq arrive there already full of fear, wanting to protect themselves at all costs, pressured by their superiors to be aggressive, act quickly, and be ready to kill at any moment.

When you are engaged in the act of killing, aware that fellow soldiers on your side are dying everyday and that it is possible for you to be killed at any moment, you are filled with fear, anger, and despair. In this state, you can become extremely cruel. You may pour all of your hate and anger on to prisoners of war by torturing and abusing them. The purpose of your violence is not primarily to extract information from them, but to express your hate and fear. The prisoners of war are the victims, but the abusers, the torturers, are also the victims. Their actions will continue to disturb them long after the abuse has ended.

Even if the superiors of the individual soldiers have not directly given orders to mistreat, abuse, or torture, they are still responsible for what happened. Preparing for war and fighting a war means allowing our human nature to die.

DEFENDING OURSELVES WITHOUT VIOLENCE

There are many other ways to defend ourselves: through diplomatic foreign policy, forming alliances with other countries, humanitarian assistance. These are all approaches motivated by the wisdom of interbeing. When we use these approaches to resolve conflicts, the army doesn't have to do much. They can serve the people by building bridges and roads and mediating small conflicts. This is not idealistic thinking; armies have worked this way in the past. With good foreign policy, the army will not have to fight.

Of course, when a country is invaded, the army should resist and defend the people. It is also sometimes necessary for other countries to help a country that is being invaded. But that is quite different from attacking other countries out of national interest. The only really necessary and appropriate circumstance under which an army should resort to violence is to physically defend itself or an ally from a direct invasion. And even in this case, much suffering will result.

Military action can be compassionate, but the compassion must be *real* compassion. If compassion is only a screen masking anger and fear, it is useless. It upsets me that former generations have committed the same mistakes and yet we don't learn from them. We haven't learned enough from the war in Vietnam. There were so many atrocities committed there. So many innocent people were tortured and killed because they were perceived as either "communist" or "anticommunist."

Mindfulness has so many layers. When we kill because we think that the other person is evil and that killing them will bring peace, we are not practicing Right Mindfulness. If we are mindful, we will see beyond the present situation to the root and the future consequences of our act in that moment. If we are truly mindful, other insights will arise: "This person I want to kill is a living being. Is there any chance for him to behave better and change his present, harmful state of mind? Maybe I have a wrong perception and one day I will see that he is just a victim of misunderstanding, and not really the evil person I think he is." Mindfulness can help a soldier to see that he may just be an instrument for killing being used by his government.

A general who is mindful of his actions is capable of looking deeply. He may not need to use weapons. He will see that there are many ways to deter the opposite side and he will exhaust all other means before resorting to violence. When nothing else works, he may use violence, but out of compassion, not out of anger.

PRESERVING OUR HUMANITY

Some soldiers are able to remain compassionate, treating prisoners and others kindly, despite their military training. These individuals are lucky enough to have received a spiritual heritage of kindness and goodness that stays at least partially intact, even through their training. This heritage is transmitted by parents, teachers, and community. Their humanity is preserved to some extent even if they have been damaged during their training. So they are still able to be shocked by their fellow soldiers' acts of torture and perhaps to practice Right Action and alert the world to the torture that is being committed. But many soldiers don't have this spiritual heritage. They come from families with much suffering and have already experienced violence and oppression before entering the army. For most people, it is possible to lose all their humanity in the process of military training.

Compassionate killing can only be done by bodhisattvas, awakened beings. In combat situations, the majority of us kill because we are afraid of being killed. So most of us are not capable of killing out of love. When our dog or horse that we love very much is suffering from a terminal sickness, we are capable of killing it to stop it from suffering. We are motivated by love. But most people in our army aren't motivated in this way. The best is to not kill at all. When you kill for your country, to defend your fellow citizens, it isn't good, but still it is better than invading other countries in the name of democracy and freedom. History has shown us that the countries the U.S. has invaded to "help" have not become more democratic and free. Prime Minister Tony Blair said that the U.K. is committed to democracy and freedom in Iraq. If we use this kind of justification, we could invade many countries because there are many that do not have enough freedom and democracy, including our own.

TORTURE IS NEVER JUSTIFIED

There is no "good cause" for torture. As a torturer, you are the first to be a victim because you lose all your humanity. You do harm to yourself in the act of harming another. If you had a good cause to begin with, it is lost when you torture another human being. No cause can justify this kind of violence.

When we imagine situations where torture could be justified, we jump to conclusions too quickly and too easily; it is not so simple. Torturing someone will not always give us the result we wish for. If the prisoner in custody does not tell us the information we want, it is because they don't want their people, their fellow soldiers to be killed. They withhold information out of compassion, out of faithfulness to their cause. Sometimes they give out wrong information and sometimes they really don't know anything. And there are those who prefer to die rather than give in to the torture.

I am absolutely against torture. Other forms of pressure or firmness may be acceptable, but not torture. When we have fear and anger in us, it is very easy to create a pretext for torturing a prisoner. When we have compassion, we can always find another way. When you torture a living being, you die as a human being because their suffering is your own suffering. When you perform surgery on someone, you know the surgery will help him and that is why you can cut into his body. But when you cut into someone's body and mind to get information from them, you cut into your own life, you kill yourself. Your life is no longer worth living. We must look at why we are engaged in war and how we have become involved in things like this. So the problem is long-term, not just looking at the immediate situation of torture.

We have to learn how to prevent situations from escalating to this point. We can do things every day to create more peaceful and harmonious relations with other countries and other peoples. Why do we wait until the situation is so bad, and then say we have to resort to the most atrocious means to stop it? We can do much better by taking care of the conflict compassionately from the very beginning.

People usually think in extreme terms of absolute nonviolence and violence, but there are many shades of gray in between. The way we talk, eat, walk can be violent. We are not dogmatic, worshiping the idea of nonviolence, because absolute nonviolence is impossible. But it is always possible to be less violent. When we have understanding and compassion in us, we have a good chance. When we are motivated by fear and anger, we are already victims. No cause is worthy enough to be served by this state of being. A truly good cause is always motivated by compassion.

Our Collective Karma

An act of cruelty is born of many conditions coming together, not by any separate, individual actor. When we hold retreats for war veterans, I tell them they are the flame at the tip of the candle—they are the ones who feel the heat, but the whole candle is burning, not only the flame. All of us are responsible.

The very ideas of terrorism and imagined weapons of mass destruction are already the result of a collective mentality, a collective way of thinking and speaking. The media helped the war happen by supporting these ideas through speech and writing. Thought, speech, and action are all collective karma.

No one can say they are not responsible for this current situation, even if we oppose our country's actions. We are still members of our community, citizens of our country. Maybe we have not done enough. We must ally ourselves with bodhisattvas, great awakened beings, who are around us, in order to transform our way of thinking and that of our society. Because wrong thinking is at the base of our present situation, thinking that has no wisdom or compassion. And we can do things every day, in every moment of our daily life to nourish the seeds of peace, compassion, and understanding in us and in those around us. We can live in such a way that can heal our collective karma and ensure that these atrocities will not happen again in the future.

Don't be tempted to use the army to solve conflicts. The only situation in which we use the army is to defend our country during an invasion. But even in this circumstance we should not rely heavily on the army; we must find other ways to protect ourselves. In the past, the U.S. was loved by many of us in the world because the U.S. represented freedom, democracy, peace, and care for other countries. The U.S. has lost this image and must rebuild it.

In the past, when I would go to the U.S. Embassy for a visa, it was not heavily guarded. But now, all over the world, American embassies are surrounded by tight security and heavily armed guards. Fear has overtaken us. It's the primary motivation for many of the U.S. government's actions, because we don't know how to protect ourselves with compassion. Students of political science must learn this in university so that they can bring real wisdom into politics. Compassion is not naive or stupid; it goes hand-in-hand with intelligence. Love is the same; real love is born from understanding.

A Knife to Kill or Chop Vegetables

Soldiers from armies around the world have asked me how to reconcile their desire for mindfulness and peace with their occupations as soldiers. If, as a soldier, you have understanding and compassion in you, then military force may help prevent something or achieve something. But that shouldn't keep us from seeing that there are other kinds of force that may be even more powerful. We don't know how to recognize and make use of these methods so we always have cause to resort to military force. The spiritual force is also very powerful. It is much safer to use the powerful spiritual, social, and educational forces. Because we have not been trained to use these forces, we only think of using military force.

Suppose there are two people, both of them full of anger, misunderstanding, and hatred. How can these two people talk to each other, and how can they negotiate for peace? That is the main problem: you cannot bring people together to sit around a table and discuss peace if there is no peace inside of them. You have to first help them to calm down and begin to see clearly that we and the other people suffer. We should have compassion for ourselves and for them and their children. This is possible. As human beings we have suffered, so we have the capacity to understand the suffering of other people.

The spiritual and educational dimensions can be very powerful, and we should use them as instruments, tools for peace. For example, suppose you live in a quarter or a village where Palestinians live peacefully with Israelis. You don't have any problems. You share the same environment, you go shopping in the same place, you ride on the same bus, you enjoy. You don't see your differences as obstacles, but as enriching. You are an Israeli and she is a Palestinian and you meet each other in the marketplace and you smile to each other. How beautiful, how wonderful. You help her and she helps you. Such places exist, and such images should be seen by other Palestinians and Israelis. The same thing is true with Iraqis and Americans, with Pakistanis and Indians.

If you are a writer you can bring that image to many people outside of your group. If you are a filmmaker, why don't you offer an image of peaceful coexistence to the world? You can televise it to demonstrate that it is possible for two groups that have fought to live peacefully and happily together. That is the work of education. There are a lot of people in the mass media who are ready to help you bring that image, that message to the world. That is very powerful—more powerful than a bomb, a rocket, or a gun—and it makes people believe that peace is possible.

If you have enough energy of understanding and peace inside of you, then this kind of educational work can be very powerful, and you won't have to think of the army and of guns anymore. If the army knows how to practice, it will know how to act in such a way as to not cause harm. The army can rescue people; the army can guarantee peace and order. It is like a knife. You can use a knife to kill or you can use a knife to chop vegetables. It is possible for soldiers to practice nonviolence and understanding. We don't exclude them from our practice, from our Sangha. We don't say, "You are a soldier, you cannot come into our meditation hall." In fact, you need to come into the meditation hall in order to know how to better use the army, how to better be in the army. So, please don't limit your question to such a small area. Make your question broad—embrace the whole situation—because everything is linked to everything else.

Every bit of our understanding, compassion, and peace is useful; it is gold. There are many things we can do today to increase these capacities in ourselves. When you take a step, if you can enjoy that step, if your step can bring you more stability and freedom, then you are serving the world. It is with that kind of peace and stability that you can serve. If you don't have the qualities of stability, peace, and freedom inside of you, then no matter what you do, you cannot help the world. It is not about "doing" something, it's about "being" something—being peace, being hope, being solid—every action will come out of that, because peace, stability, and freedom always seek a way to express themselves in action.

That is the spiritual dimension of our reality. We need that spiritual dimension to rescue us so that we don't think only in terms of military force as a means to solve the problem and uproot terrorism. How can you uproot terrorism with military force? The military doesn't know where terrorism is. They cannot locate terrorism—it is in the heart. The more military force you use, the more terrorists you create, in your own country and in other countries as well.

The basic issue is our practice of peace, our practice of looking deeply. First of all, we need to allow ourselves to calm down. Without tranquility and serenity, our emotions, anger, and despair will not go away, and we will not be able to look and see the nature of reality. Calming down, becoming serene is the first step of meditation. The second step is to look deeply to understand. Out of understanding comes compassion. And from this foundation of understanding and compassion, you will be able to see what you can do and what you should refrain from doing. This is meditation. Every one of us has to practice meditation—the politicians, the military, the businessmen. All of us have to practice calming down and looking deeply. You have the support of all of us in doing this.

MINDFUL CONSEQUENCES

Of course it is very difficult to not get angry when someone is killing your wife, your husband, or your children. It is very difficult to not get angry. That person is acting out of anger, and we are retaliating also out of anger. So there is not much difference between the two of us. That is the first element.

The second element is, why do we have to wait until the situation presents itself to us as an emergency before we act, dealing only with the immediate circumstance? Of course you have to act rapidly in such an emergency situation. But what if we are not in an emergency situation? We can wait for an emergency situation to arise or we can do something in order to prevent such a thing from happening. Our tendency is not to do anything until the worst happens. While we have the time, we do not know how to use that time to practice peace and prevent war. We just allow ourselves to indulge in forgetfulness and sense pleasures. We do not do the things that have the power to prevent such emergency situations from happening.

The third element is that when things like this happen, it is because there is a deep-seated cause, not only in the present moment but also in the past. This is because that is. Nothing happens without a cause. You kill me, I kill you. But the fact that you are killing me and I am killing you has its roots in the past and will have an effect on the future. Our children will say, "You killed my grandfather, now I have to kill you." That can go on for a long time. When you get angry, when you have so much hatred towards the person who has made you suffer, and when you are willing to use any means to destroy him, you are acting out of anger just like he is. And anger is not the only cause. There are also misunderstandings, wrong perceptions about each other, and there are people who urge us to kill the other side because otherwise we will not be safe. There are many causes.

In the past our fathers and our grandfathers may not have been very mindful and may have said things and done things that have sown seeds of war. And their grandfathers also said things and did things, planting seeds of war. And now our generation has a choice. Do we want to do better than our grandfathers, or do we want to repeat exactly what they did? That is the legacy we will leave for our children and grandchildren.

Of course in a situation of great emergency you have to do everything you can to prevent killing. And yet, there are ways to do it that will cause less harm. If you have some compassion and understanding, the way you do it can be very different. Bring the dimension of the human heart into it; help the military strategists to have a human heart. It's the least we can do. Do we teach the military to conduct a military operation with a human heart? Is that a reality in the army, in military schools? They teach us how to kill as many people as possible and as quickly as possible, but they do not teach us how to kill someone with compassion.

In one of his past lives, it seems that the Buddha was a passenger on a boat that was overtaken by pirates, and he killed one of them while trying to protect the people on the boat. But that was in an earlier life of the Buddha, before he was an awakened being. If the true Buddha were there he may have had other means; he may have had enough wisdom to find a better way so that the life of the pirate could have been spared. Because in life after life, the Buddha made progress. You are the afterlife of your grandfather; you must have learned something over the past three generations. If you don't have more compassion and understanding than he did, then you have not properly continued your grandfather. Because with compassion and understanding we can do better, we can cause less harm, and create more peace.

We cannot expect to achieve one hundred percent peace right away—our degree of understanding and love is not yet deep enough. But in every situation, urgent or not, the elements of understanding and compassion can play a role. When a gangster is trying to beat and kill, of course you have to lock him up so he will not cause more harm. But you can lock him up angrily, with a lot of hate, or you can lock him up with compassion and with the idea that we should do something to help him. In that case, prison becomes a place where there is love and help. You have to teach the prison guards how to look at the prisoners with compassionate eyes. Teach them how to treat the prisoners with tenderness so they will suffer less in prison, so we can better help them. Do we train them to look at prisoners with eyes of compassion? Perhaps a prisoner has killed, has destroyed. Maybe he was raised in such a way that killing and destruction were natural for him, and so he is a victim of society, of his family, and his education. If, as a prison guard, you look and see him in that way, then you will have compassion and understanding, and treat your prisoner with more gentleness. When you help this person to become a better person, you help yourself to be happy.

We should not focus only on short-term action. Again, we have to look with the eyes of the Buddha. We must train ourselves to look at things with a broad perspective and not just concentrate on the immediacy of the problem. That is what our lives are for, and so are the lives of our children. We are a continuation of each other. We build synagogues, churches, and mosques in order to have a place to sit down and do that—to look deeply, so that our actions will not only be motivated by desire, greed, or anger. We have a chance to sit in the mosque, the church or synagogue for a long time, and in that time our compassion and understanding should grow. And then we will know how to act in the world in a better way, for the cause of peace.

As a soldier you can be compassionate. You can be loving and your gun can be helpful. There are times you may not have to use your gun. It is like that knife that is used to cut vegetables. You can be a bodhisattva as a soldier or as a commander of the army. The question is whether you have understanding and compassion in your heart. That is the question.

CHAPTER THREE

Nourishing Peace

THE BUDDHA SPOKE about the path of emancipation in terms of consumption. In The Discourse on the Son's Flesh the Buddha taught that we consume four kinds of nutriments. If every day we are aware of what we are consuming and understand its nature, we can transform the suffering inside us and around us. Consuming with awareness is essential to ending terrorism.

THE FIRST NUTRIMENT: EDIBLE FOOD

The first kind of nutriment the Buddha spoke about is the food we eat. He advised us to eat mindfully so that compassion can be maintained in our heart. The foods we eat can bring poisons into our body that can destroy our compassion. They can cause suffering in our body, our mind, and in the world. Therefore, we have to know what we are eating and whether the food we eat is destroying us and destroying our planet.

To illustrate this, the Buddha told a story of a young couple and their three-year-old son who had to cross a vast desert to move to another country. Halfway through the desert they ran out of food, and they knew they would die if they couldn't find food. Out of desperation they decided to kill their little boy and eat his flesh. They ate a small piece of his flesh and preserved the rest by carrying it on their shoulders and letting it dry in the sun. Every time they ate a piece of their son's flesh they cried out in despair, "Where is our beloved son now?" They beat their chests and pulled their hair. They suffered tremendously. Finally they were able to cross the desert and enter the other land, but they continued to suffer, mourning their little boy.

After telling this story, the Buddha asked his monks, "Dear friends, do you think the couple enjoyed eating the flesh of their son?" The monks answered, "No, how could anyone enjoy eating the flesh of their own son?" The Buddha said, "If we do not consume mindfully we are eating the flesh of our own son or daughter."

For most of us, the body we received at birth was a healthy one, but if we consume unmindfully and eat foods that bring about illness in our body and mind, we are destroying the body we have been given. We are unkind to our ancestors. Our body has been handed down to us by many generations and we have no right to destroy it by the way we eat and drink.

If we use drugs, drink alcohol, or smoke cigarettes, we are consuming poisons that destroy our body and mind. We are eating the flesh of our father, our mother, and our ancestors. We are also eating the flesh of our children and our children's children because this body that we are destroying is what we will hand down to our children and future generations. People tend to think, "This is my body, I can do anything I want. It is my life." But our body does not belong to us alone; it belongs to our ancestors, our family, and our children as well. Your body is the continuation of your ancestors. You have to take good care of it so you can transmit your best to your children and your grandchildren, your partner, and your community.

When we eat meat and drink alcohol we eat our children's flesh. Even the production of alcohol creates suffering. Alcohol production requires grain that could be used to feed the starving people in the world. To make one glass of rice wine takes a whole basket of rice that could feed hungry children.[3] Eighty percent of the corn and ninety-five percent of the oats in the United States are fed to animals raised for humans to eat. The oatmeal we humans eat in the morning is only five percent of the oatmeal grown in the United States. The world's cattle alone consume a quantity of food equivalent to the caloric needs of 8.7 billion people, more than the entire human population on Earth.

There are so many people who are dying of hunger in the world. The United Nations International Children's Emergency Fund (UNICEF) reports that every day 40,000 children die of malnutrition. Meanwhile, many of us in the West overeat. Fifty-five percent of Americans are overweight. Obesity is fast becoming a national health hazard. When we overeat, we destroy our own body, and the body of our ancestors and our descendants. A French economist once told me that if overdeveloped countries in the West reduced their meat and alcohol consumption by fifty percent, we could solve the problem of hunger in the world.

Emory College reports the following on the environmental impact of U.S. meat production:

✦ Land: Of all agricultural land in the U.S., 87 percent is used to raise animals for food. That is 45 percent of the total landmass in the U.S.

---

3 The statistics in this paragraph are from Emory College's Green Book, 2003. http://students.edu.ECOSEAC/greenbook/eating.htm.

✦ Water: More than half of all the water consumed in the U.S. for all purposes is used to raise animals for food. It takes 2,500 gallons of water to produce a pound of meat. It takes 25 gallons of water to produce a pound of wheat. That is 25 versus 2,500 gallons of water. A totally vegetarian diet requires 300 gallons of water per day, while a meat-based diet requires 4,000 gallons of water per day.

✦ Pollution: Raising animals for food causes more water pollution in the U.S. than any other industry. Animals raised for food produce 130 times the excrement of the entire human population, 87,000 pounds per second. Much of the waste from factory farms and slaughterhouses flows into streams and rivers, contaminating water sources.

✦ Deforestation: Each vegetarian saves an acre of trees every year. More than 260 million acres of U.S. forests have been cleared to grow crops to feed animals raised for meat. An acre of trees disappears every eight seconds. The tropical rain forests are being destroyed to create grazing land for cattle. Fifty-five square feet of rain forest may be cleared to produce just one quarter-pound burger.

The forests are our lungs. They give us oxygen and they protect our environment. If we eat meat, we are destroying the forests and therefore eating the flesh of our Mother Earth. All of us, including children, have the capacity to see the suffering of animals raised for food. We can choose to eat mindfully, and to protect the happiness and lives of our fellow species and Mother Earth herself.

The way we eat even brings about war. The amount of resources we use to make meat is immense. The people in the U.S. are only six percent of the whole world's population but the resources they consume are sixty percent of all resources used on Earth. In the West, we live very luxuriously, eating far more than we need, while others are dying of hunger. We eat in such a way that we destroy the planet Earth. This is a great injustice, an offense against the entire human race, as well as animals, plants, minerals, and the atmosphere. This inequality causes hatred and anger in the world. When anger and hatred are repressed, they explode in violence.

We have the chance to stop the killing of animals, and find more nonviolent ways to produce our food. Food can be delicious without using the flesh of animals. When we eat mindfully, we maintain awareness of our interdependence with other beings and this awareness helps us maintain compassion in our heart. When we eat with compassion, happiness arises.

One way to nourish our compassion is to discuss with our family how to eat and drink with more mindfulness. Another way is, as a society, to look together at how we produce and consume food.

THE SECOND NUTRIMENT: SENSORY FOOD

The second kind of food that the Buddha spoke about is sensory impressions. We eat with our six sense organs: our eyes, ears, nose, tongue, body, and mind. A television program is food; a conversation is food; music is food; art is food; billboards are food. When you drive through the city, you consume and are penetrated by these things without your knowledge or consent. What you see, what you touch, what you hear is food.

These items of consumption can be highly toxic. There is good music and there are good magazine articles and television programs that nourish understanding and compassion in us. We should enjoy them. But many kinds of music, television programs, and magazines contain craving, despair, and violence. The television advertisements you are forced to watch are the food of sense impressions. Their whole purpose is to make you crave the products they want to sell and arouse your desire. We consume these poisons and we allow our children to consume them also, causing fear and hatred in us to grow every day. It's not a problem of consuming less or more, but of right consumption, mindful consumption.

To illustrate the importance of mindful consumption of sense impressions, the Buddha used the image of a cow with skin disease. A cow was so sick that she lost virtually all her skin and was vulnerable wherever she went. When the cow came close to a tree or an old wall, or when she entered the water, tiny creatures would come and suck her blood. The cow had no means of self-protection. If we don't know how to consume mindfully, we are like a cow without skin, the toxins of violence, despair, and craving penetrating right into the core of our being.

According to the American Psychological Association, a typical American child will watch 100,000 acts of violence and 8,000 murders on television in his lifetime. That is too much. When parents are so busy and don't have time for their children, television becomes a dangerous babysitter. From a very young age, children already begin to consume very toxic sounds and images. They become victims of violence and fear.

There are people who argue that although they watched cowboy movies when they were young, they have not grown up to be violent. But the cowboy films of the past are not the same as the movies of today. Movies of a generation ago did have some violence, but a lot less than films have now, and they communicated some sense of morality; if someone committed an act of murder, he went to prison. At least the person who committed violence couldn't get away with it. Films now often show violence without consequence or responsibility. In many video games, people are shot and killed, and then come alive again as fresh targets. When children play this kind of game every day, it is easy to understand how they end up bringing a gun to school and shooting others. This kind of game is infinitely dangerous. When children are young they cannot distinguish between the game and reality. Because children consume this kind of sensory food every day through television and video games, they are constantly feeding the violence in their consciousness.

America is getting angrier and angrier every day. More and more, we are consuming the kind of sensory food that brings violence and hatred into our bodies and minds. The energy of violence in people is being nourished everywhere in daily life. The violence in us overwhelms us and demands an outlet.

We can choose sensory food that heals and nourishes us or sensory food that poisons us. There are certain kinds of books and articles that make us feel very happy and light after we have read them. Certain music or talks may be the same; as we listen, we feel inspired and happy. We can choose to consume items that bring lightness, peace, and happiness into our body and mind.

A simple conversation with another person can lead you to utter despair or it can give you hope and confidence. Sometimes, after listening to someone talk, you feel very depressed. Conversations can contain toxins, so we have to speak and listen in mindfulness. Loneliness may push you to talk to anyone just to avoid being alone. But if someone is speaking in a very negative way, this kind of conversation can kill you. Only listen to and speak with people who nourish love and understanding in you, unless you are speaking with someone with the sole purpose of helping them to transform their suffering and violence.

The Buddha said that mindfulness is the capacity to return to what is happening in the present moment. We can be aware of what we are consuming. The way we produce and consume is destroying us, our young people, and our whole nation. Everyone of us can practice mindfulness in order to change this. As parents, schoolteachers, filmmakers, and journalists we have to observe to see whether we are contributing to the growth of violence by the way we live our daily lives. All of us must share our insight, for only our collective awakening can help us stop this course of destruction.

Our Congress, and our whole nation, can practice looking deeply into the nature of what we consume every day. We have elected Congress members and we can ask them to make laws to prohibit toxic production. We can talk with our families and communities and make a commitment to mindful, intelligent consumption of both edible foods and cultural items. Consuming mindfully is the only way to protect ourselves and our society from the violence that is overwhelming us. When we consume mindfully, we receive nourishment and healing in our daily life which allows us to embrace and transform the pain and violence in us. Then we will know what to do to make the Earth a safe place for us, our children, and their children. This is the real practice of peace.

THE THIRD NUTRIMENT: OUR DEEPEST DESIRE

The third kind of food is volition, our deepest desire. We have to ask ourselves, "What is my deepest desire in this life?" Our desire can take us in the direction of happiness or in the direction of suffering. Desire is a kind of food that nourishes us and gives us energy. If you have a healthy desire, such as a wish to protect life, to protect the environment, or live a simple life with time to take care of yourself and your beloved ones, your desire will bring you to happiness. If you run after power, wealth, sex, and fame, thinking that they will bring you happiness, you are consuming a very dangerous kind of food and it will bring you a lot of suffering. You can see this is true just by looking around you.

In 1999, at a retreat for business leaders, many people shared that those with great wealth and power also suffer tremendously. A very wealthy businessman told us of his suffering and loneliness. He owns a very large business with over 300,000 workers, operating in every part of the world, including Vietnam. He shared that people who are very rich are often extremely lonely because they are suspicious of others. They think anyone who approaches them in friendship only does so because of their money and only wants to take advantage of them. They feel they do not have any real friends. Children of wealthy people also suffer deeply; often their parents have no time for them because they are so preoccupied with maintaining their wealth.

Several years ago, at a retreat we offered in San Diego, California, two famous artists attended. One was Peter Yarrow, the folksinger from Peter, Paul and Mary, and the other was Julie Christie, the movie actress. They both told us that their fame does not make them happy. Their happiness comes from being able to come back to their own heart and mind and really practice. Odette Lara, the Brazilian film star, attended a retreat in California in the early 1980s, and afterward she wrote me a letter. "Dear Thây. I thought my tree was already dead, because for a long time I have had no desire in my heart. But this morning I woke up and suddenly felt a new desire—a new bud coming from the tree that I thought had no life."

The Buddha had a very deep desire, but it was not for money, fame, power, or sex. Siddhartha, who became the Buddha, had had enough of that when he was a prince. His desire was to transform all of his suffering, to be happy and to help other people to suffer less. He didn't want to follow his father, and become a king or a politician. The Buddha is still helping us 2,600 years later. When he became a monk, Siddhartha lived very simply; he only had three robes and a bowl and he walked everywhere. He lived like this for forty years. He brought happiness to himself and countless other people without desiring wealth, sex, power, and fame.

To illustrate the third kind of food, the Buddha gave the example of a young man who wanted very much to live but there were two strong men who wanted to kill him. They dragged him toward a pit of burning coals, and though he struggled against them, in the end they overpowered him and threw him into the pit. The Buddha said that our desire is like those two strong men. Our desires can drag us to a pit of burning coals or they can lead us to happiness, health, and peace. If you allow desire for wealth, sex, power, fame, or revenge to overwhelm you, then you are being dragged by those two strong men toward the pit of coals. Ask yourself, "Where is my desire taking me? What is its nature?" Is it for a bigger house, a better job, a degree, fame, a high position in society—or is it something deeper? Don't let your desire be small, it should be very great. If it is not a great desire you will be pulled away by many smaller desires.

Please take some time to write down your deepest desire. Do you want to live as a free person without worries or craving? The desire to be a free person is very worthwhile. To be free means you are no longer the victim of fear, anger, craving, or suspicion. Do you want this? Maybe you want it but you do not want it enough. You have other desires that get in the way, such as wanting a bigger house or a better car or tastier food. Those little desires distract you from your more noble desire. If Siddhartha's desire for freedom had not been strong, he would not have been able to overcome sensual desires. If you want to realize your deep desire, you have to really want it.

Perhaps you desire better communication with your partner. Maybe you have difficulty with your partner and you cannot look at each other anymore. Maybe you desire a closer relationship with your children. When you and your family are happy, then you have the opportunity to help other people and to help your country. Many of us want to help our country and the entire human species. But because this desire is not nurtured enough by our environment, we are easily distracted. Becoming a monastic is a bit like joining a revolution; you have to be willing to give up everything because you want liberation so much.

Cultivating Compassion

Some people spend their whole life trying only to get revenge. This kind of desire or volition will bring great suffering not only to others but to oneself as well. Hatred is a fire that burns in every soul and can only be tempered by compassion. But where do we find compassion? It isn't sold in the supermarket. If it was, we would only need to bring it home and we could solve all the hatred and violence in the world very easily. But compassion can only be produced in our own heart by our own practice.

Right now America is burning with fear, suffering, and hatred. If only to ease our suffering, we have to return to ourselves and seek to understand why we are caught up in so much violence. What has caused terrorists to hate so much that they are willing to sacrifice their own lives and create so much suffering for other people? We see their great hatred, but what lies underneath it? Injustice. Of course we have to find a way to stop their violence, we may even need to keep people locked in prison while their hatred burns. But the important thing is to look deeply and ask, "What responsibility do we have for the injustice in the world?"

Sometimes someone we love—our child, our spouse, or our parent—says or does something cruel and we suffer and get angry. We think it is only we who suffer. But the other person is suffering as well. If he wasn't suffering, he wouldn't have spoken or acted out of anger. The person we love doesn't know a way out of his suffering. This is why our beloved pours out all his hatred and violence on to us. Our responsibility is to produce the energy of compassion that calms down our own heart and allows us to help the other person. If we punish the other person, he will just suffer more.

Responding to violence with violence can only bring more violence, more injustice, and more suffering, not only to others but also to ourselves. This wisdom is in every one of us. When we breathe deeply, we can touch this seed of wisdom in us. I know that if the energy of wisdom and of compassion in the American people could be nourished for even one week, it would reduce the level of anger and hatred in the country. I urge all of us to practice calming and concentrating our minds, watering the seeds of wisdom and compassion that are already in us, and learning the art of mindful consumption. If we can do this, we will create a true peaceful revolution, the only kind of revolution that can help us get out of this difficult situation.

Some people may think the life of a monastic is mysterious. But in the monastery, all we do is practice producing compassion and looking at all species with the eyes of compassion and love. To do this, we have to be very careful of what we consume. Whether we are eating a bowl of rice, enjoying a field of flowers, or nourishing our deepest desire, we practice doing it as mindfully as possible, conscious of each breath.

THE FOURTH NUTRIMENT: CONSCIOUSNESS

The fourth kind of food is consciousness. In Buddhism we speak of consciousness as having two levels. The lower level is called store consciousness and the upper level is called mind consciousness.

When we think, calculate or dream, we are working on the level of the mind consciousness. The mind consciousness is like a living room. Underneath it is a very big basement, the store consciousness. Everything you don't like you stuff down in the basement. Store consciousness stores everything in the form of seeds. And just like in the earth, if you water those seeds, they sprout.

Fifty-one kinds of seeds, both wholesome and unwholesome, live in the store consciousness. Wholesome seeds are seeds of love, forgiveness, generosity, happiness, joy. Unwholesome seeds include hatred, discrimination, and craving. According to Buddhist psychology, when these seeds manifest they are called mental formations. For example, our anger is a mental formation. When it is not manifesting, we do not feel angry. But this doesn't mean that the seed of anger is not in us. All of us have the seed of anger lying in our basement, our store consciousness. We can play and have fun and we don't feel angry at all, but if someone comes along and waters the seed of anger in our store consciousness, it will begin to sprout and come up into our living room. In the beginning it was just a seed but once it has been watered, it arises and becomes the mental formation of anger, taking away all our happiness.

The Buddha used the following image to illustrate the fourth kind of nutriment. A criminal was arrested. The king gave the order to stab him with one hundred knives. The criminal did not die. The same punishment was repeated at noon, and in the evening. Still, he did not die. The punishment was repeated the next day, and the day that followed. In the same way, we allow ourselves to be stabbed hundreds of times a day by negative mental formations. When any seed manifests in our mind consciousness, we absorb it and this is what is called consciousness food, the fourth nutriment. If we allow anger to come up into our mind consciousness and stay for a whole hour, for that whole hour we are eating anger. The more we eat anger, the more the seed of anger grows. If the seed of loving kindness arises in your mind consciousness, and you can keep it there for a whole hour, then during that time you are consuming a whole hour of loving kindness.

Selective Watering

We can help each other water the wholesome seeds in our store consciousness. We can say to those close to us, "Dear one, let's be careful not to water the unwholesome seeds in each other. Let's water only the wholesome seeds in each other and then we can have nourishing food for our consciousness." When we water seeds of forgiveness, acceptance, and happiness in the person we love, we are giving them very healthy food for their consciousness, as if we were cooking them a delicious healthy meal. But if we constantly water the seed of hatred, craving, and anger in our loved one, we are poisoning them.

We could sit down with our family and even write out an agreement that everyone can sign together, committing to watering the wholesome seeds in each other. If we can practice in this way, then our children can practice, too. An agreement like this could be the foundation of our happiness. If you nourish yourself with the four nutriments, consuming a healthy diet of edible food, sensations, desires, and mental formations, then you and your loved ones will benefit in concrete ways. Buddhism becomes not just abstract teachings, but something that changes your daily life.

The Buddha said, "Nothing can survive without food." This is a very simple and very deep truth. Love and hate are both living things. If you do not nourish your love, it will die. If you cut the source of nutriment for your violence, your violence will die. If you want your love to last, you have to give it food every day. Love cannot live without food. If you neglect your love, after a while it will die and hatred may take its place. Do you know how to nourish your love?

If we don't give hatred food, it too will die. Hatred and suffering grow greater every day because every day we nourish them, giving them more food. With what kind of food have you nourished your despair and your hatred? If you are depressed, you may have no strength and no energy left. You may feel that you want to die. Why do you feel like that? Our depression doesn't just come out of nowhere. If we can recognize the food that has nourished our depression, we can stop consuming it. Within a few weeks our depression will die of starvation. If you don't know that you are watering your depression, you will continue to do it every day. The Buddha said that if we know how to look deeply into our suffering and recognize what feeds it, we are already on the path of emancipation.

The way out of our suffering is mindfulness of consumption, not only for ourselves but for the whole world. If we know how to water the seeds of wisdom and compassion in us, these seeds become powerful sources of energy helping us to forgive those who have hurt us. This will bring relief to our nation and to our world. The American people are capable of realizing this kind of wisdom and compassion.

CHAPTER FOUR

Leading with Courage and Compassion

PEACE IS MADE OF PEACE

IN THE FALL OF 2003, I offered a public talk at the Library of Congress and a weekend retreat for U.S. Congress members to help them build an inner island of peace and stability to better face the demands of political life. I shared how we can create more time to be present for ourselves, to release the tension in our bodies and minds, and touch the wonders of life within and around us. In the retreat, Congress members practiced sitting peacefully together, walking mindfully, and eating meals with mindfulness and gratitude. They saw that the practice of mindfulness is a concrete expression of our peace, stability, and freedom. Peace is made of peace. Peace is a living substance we build our lives with. It is not only made of discussions and treaties. To infuse our world with peace, we must walk in peace, speak with peace, and listen with peace. If we do this, we will be able to bring more joy into our daily lives, relate better to our family members, and use our insight, compassion, and understanding to better serve our community and be able to help heal the wounds that divide our nation and the world.

When you sit at the airport, use this time to go home to yourself and take care of your body and mind. Instead of allowing yourself to worry about the future, practice mindful breathing to return to the present moment. We breathe in and out all day but we are not aware that we are breathing in and breathing out. Wherever we are, in traffic waiting for a red light to change, we can bring our attention to our breath. "Breathing in, I know I am breathing in. Breathing out, I know I am breathing out. Breathing in, I know I am alive. Breathing out, I smile to life."

This is a very simple practice. If we go home to our in-breath and out-breath, breathing in and out mindfully, we become fully present, fully alive in the here and now. In daily life, our minds are often elsewhere—in the past or in the future, caught in our projects, our worries, and our anxieties. When our minds are not with our bodies, we aren't truly present, and we can't touch life deeply. Life is only available in the present moment. The past is already gone, the future is not yet here. We have an appointment with life and it is right now.

We don't have to wait until we die to go to the Kingdom of Heaven; in fact, we have to be very alive. The Buddhist equivalent of the Kingdom of Heaven is the Pure Land of the Buddha. This is not a place we get to by dying or becoming martyrs for our faith. The Kingdom of God isn't just an idea; it's a reality, available to us in the full moon, the blue sky, the majestic mountains and rivers, and the beautiful faces of our children. We need only to be present, to breathe in and out mindfully, in order to get in touch with the Kingdom of God. The Kingdom of God is always available to us. But are we available to the Kingdom?

When we come home to the present moment, we become aware of our body, and all of our tension is released. Everyone can practice paying attention to their breath, perhaps repeating these words, "Breathing in, I am aware of my body. Breathing out, I release the tension in my body." You don't need to be a Buddhist to practice this. You can sit in whatever position you feel comfortable and practice releasing the tension and tightness in your body. One or two minutes of practice can already make a big difference. When I breathe in, I generate the energy of mindfulness. With this energy, I recognize my body's aches and tensions, I begin to embrace my body tenderly, and allow any tension to be released. Many of us accumulate a lot of tension and pressure in our bodies, working them too hard. It's time to come home to our bodies. This is possible any time, whether we are sitting, lying, standing, or walking.

The practice of walking mindfully is possible for every one of us, whether we are at home, at the airport, or on Capitol Hill. Each step made in mindfulness is very nourishing and healing, and brings solidity and freedom. When I walk in mindfulness, I do not think. If you think while you walk, you will be lost in your thinking and you cannot enjoy making steps, walking in the Kingdom of God, the Pure Land of the Buddha. With the energy of mindfulness and concentration, you can enjoy every step you make. Practicing mindful walking with a friend or a community can make it much easier, but alone it may be more difficult. Perhaps you can invite a partner, a friend, or a coworker to practice with you.

Being Fully Present

Coming home to our bodies can bring us relief within just a few minutes. After that, we come home to our feelings and emotions. "Breathing in, I am aware of my feelings. Breathing out, I calm and release the tension in my feelings." This kind of practice can be done anytime, anywhere, on a train, on an airplane, at work, or at home.

If we do not know how to take care of ourselves and to love ourselves, we cannot take care of the people we love. Loving oneself is the foundation for loving another person. If we love someone, the greatest gift we can make to him or to her is our true presence. If we are caught in our thinking and our worries about the past and the future, we aren't truly present, and so we can't offer this most precious thing, our presence and compassion, to our loved ones. Breathing and walking mindfully, and becoming fully alive should be our top priority.

How can you love if you aren't really present? To love someone is a practice. If you're really there, your beloved will know it. If you only pretend to be there, your loved one will know that as well. When you bring your mind back to your body and become fully present in the here and now, you're in a position to take care of your beloved one. Your own presence in the here and now will make life available to you. Your beloved belongs to life. The Kingdom of God belongs to life. When you become present, your beloved one and the Kingdom of God become available to you at the same time.

When I drink tea with my full awareness, this is mindful drinking. If I establish myself in the here and now, my tea becomes fully present, too. It is possible to drink our tea and eat our breakfast mindfully. You might ask: "I have so many things to take care of and think about, how can I afford the time to drink my tea mindfully?" But if you are lost in your thinking while you drink your tea, it isn't true tea drinking. You are not real and the tea is not real. This is why non-thinking is a very important practice. I don't deny that thinking is important. But there is productive thinking and unproductive thinking. If we aren't capable of living the moments of our daily life deeply, we can't touch reality in a deep way and our thinking won't be very productive. I usually enjoy walking meditation before I give a talk. While walking to the auditorium, I don't think about my talk. I just enjoy every step I make. This is why when the time comes for the talk, the talk can be good. The time of non-talking is the foundation for the time of talking.

Embracing Our Pain

Coming home to ourselves so that we can recognize our pain, sorrow, fear, and anger is a fundamental practice. Mindfulness and concentration help us to do this without the fear of being overwhelmed by these negative energies. Many of us are afraid of being with ourselves because we're afraid of the huge amount of fear, loneliness, and anger in us. This is why we seek to cover up and avoid these blocks of suffering by consuming food, television, books, and alcohol. With the energy born from mindful breathing and mindful walking, it is possible to get in touch with our pain without being overwhelmed by it.

The energy of mindfulness helps us to recognize our pain and embrace it tenderly like a mother whose baby is crying. When the baby cries, the mother stops whatever she is doing, goes to pick up her baby, and holds it tenderly in her arms. The energy of the mother penetrates into the baby and the baby begins to feel better immediately. When we recognize and embrace the pain and sorrow within us, it calms down like the baby in her mother's arms.

If we hold our anger, sorrow, and fear with mindfulness, we will be able to recognize the roots of our afflictions. With mindfulness, we can also recognize the suffering in the person we love. If he speaks or acts in a hurtful way, we can understand that he is a victim of suffering that he doesn't know how to handle. This awareness makes us want to help him to transform his suffering as we have transformed our own.

Once we taste true happiness and peace, it's very easy to transform our anger. We don't have to fight anymore. Our anger begins to dissolve because we're able to bring elements of peace and joy into our body and consciousness every day. Mindfulness helps us avoid bringing elements of war and violence into our body and consciousness. This basic practice can transform the anger, fear, and violence within us so that we can better serve ourselves and our country.

Members of Congress probably want to offer the best of their insight, experience, and understanding to their country. But because they belong to a certain party, they have to vote according to its interests and may not always be able to vote according to their own insight. This is unwise political action. When people elect someone to Congress, they rely on that person's wisdom, talent, and experience. The title of the retreat I gave for members of Congress was "Leading with Courage and Compassion." Leading requires, first of all, voting with courage and being willing to risk losing status in a political party. Sometimes politicians do not dare express their thoughts or insights out of fear they will be ostracized. This is a big problem. With enough mindfulness and concentration, politicians could understand the suffering and the difficulties of their constituents. With this understanding, they can offer the kind of insight that will respond effectively to the situation, regardless of their political party.

But for the most part in Congress, our representatives just fight for their ideas. They don't listen to each other. Any idea that doesn't correspond to the political party's platform is considered wrong. If people from another party share a real, valuable insight, politicians have to reject it. Each politician's goal is to defend their party's positions. Colleagues in other parties are considered adversaries or even enemies. If you're caught in this way of reacting, there's no possibility for real communication and mutual understanding in Congress. This isn't real democracy. This is a threat to democracy. The current quality of listening and speaking in Congress isn't very good. If Congress could practice deep listening and loving speech, it would become a family, a community.

In Plum Village, we have developed a practice called Beginning Anew to keep communication open and restore love and understanding in the community. Although it would be difficult at first, using this process in Congress would change the whole way this country engages in politics.

Once each week, we sit together in a circle with a vase of flowers in the center and we practice loving speech and listening deeply to each other. We invite the bell of mindfulness to begin and to end, also after each person has spoken, and whenever it is needed. When someone wants to speak, she goes to the center, picks up the vase of flowers, and brings it back to her place. She sits with the flowers in front of her, and they help her maintain her freshness as she speaks. While she is speaking, no one may interrupt.

She begins with "flower watering," recognizing the wholesome and wonderful qualities of others in the community. Each person has positive qualities, and with a little awareness we can recognize them. This is a chance to encourage and appreciate others and to be in touch with the gratitude we feel.

After watering the flowers, she may express regret for any unskillfulness, any mistake she has made, or any hurt she may have caused. She may also express if she has felt hurt by someone in the community.

This can be the first step toward reconciliation. Beginning with flower watering is very important. It is difficult to hold on to anger and resentment when we are aware of the other person's beautiful qualities and we have a larger, more balanced view of them. She speaks truthfully and constructively, without blaming, arguing, or criticizing. Her aim is not to divide, but to strengthen and heal the community. Everyone, including the person who has hurt her, listens deeply without judging or reacting, giving her a chance to express herself and have some relief. If he were to respond to her in that moment, she would not feel she was being heard. Listening in this way is a very deep practice. It takes skill and patience, and it is very important.

If the other person would like to respond to her with the whole community present, he will have the opportunity at the next session of Beginning Anew. If she simply has a misperception that he would like to clear up, he can go to her privately in a few days and tell her sweetly and calmly that she was not correct. If they would like to meet, they can arrange a time and ask others to be present or they can ask a third person to be there as a mediator.

Last, the speaker has the opportunity to reveal any situation, difficulty, or happiness affecting her right now that she would like to share with the community. When she has finished speaking, she returns the vase of flowers to the center, goes back to her seat and another person then has the opportunity to take a turn and speak.

We close the session with a song or by holding hands with everyone in the circle and breathing together for a minute. After Beginning Anew, everyone in the community feels light. Even if we have only taken the first steps toward healing, we know that we can continue. Congress right now is often filled with recriminations, with fighting and posturing. If politicians could practice Beginning Anew, space for truth and healing might open up.

FIVE STEPS FOR COMING HOME TO OURSELVES

Public figures often express their concern about the increasing level of violence in our society. They're right; there is far too much violence in our families and in our schools. Each politician may have ideas and insights about how to reduce violence. But instead of sharing ideas, politicians compete to have their own idea prevail. If instead, we can combine all our individual insights and experiences, we will arrive at a collective insight. If we are not capable of listening to our colleagues with an open heart simply because they belong to another political party—and we only consider and support ideas from our own party as worthwhile—we are harming the very foundation of democracy.

To transform Congress into a compassionate community of true brothers and sisters—where everyone learns to listen to everyone else with equal interest and concern—is a very deep practice and the first step would be for each politician to come home to herself. Most politicians haven't had time to come home to themselves. They are constantly focused outside of themselves. They are rarely in touch with or taking care of their bodies, feelings, mental formations, and consciousness. They allow themselves to be carried away by things around them, like their projects, worries, regrets, or by meaningless entertainment. So, the first step is to go home to yourself and to recognize the suffering, the pain in you, and to know how to embrace and transform it.

After coming home to themselves, I recommended that each politician approach her family, her partner. Once you have gone home to yourself, you are in a position to help a partner go home to him or herself, to heal the pain they have inside. This is the second step; taking care of your beloved.

When you have succeeded in the first and second steps, you and your partner become one. You can share your concerns, your aspirations, and your difficulties with your partner and your family, and all of you become stronger. If you don't include your partner in your mindfulness, he becomes an obstacle. And you become an obstacle for him. When you have the support of your family and there is good communication, you no longer feel lonely and you have plenty of happiness. Then you have the energy to pursue your dreams.

I recommended that once each politician has united with his family, he could take a third step and help the people who work in his office to go back to themselves. Every senator, every representative, has staff members. They have their own suffering and difficulties. How a congressperson speaks and acts toward them may contribute in some way to their suffering. This is why taking care of members of your staff is very important. Listen to them using the techniques of deep listening and loving speech to create mutual understanding and trust. You can only succeed as a leader when you have a staff that has confidence in you and supports you.

When, through your own practice, you can inspire your staff to go home to themselves, they will work not just for money but because they want to realize a shared ideal. This is a very healthy kind of desire. This is true whether you are a politician, a businessperson, or anyone who works with other people. If you don't know anything about the difficulties, suffering, and aspirations of the people who work with you, then they can't be with you one hundred percent. When you work together as a team, as a community, then you are in a much stronger position to take the fourth and the fifth steps.

The fourth healing step I recommended is that congressional representatives listen to their colleagues. Every member of Congress has his or her own difficulties and aspirations. The most meaningful thing a member of Congress could do is to offer her best insight and talent, and listen to the wisdom of others.

There is far too much division, suspicion, and hatred in Congress. With so much division and enmity, it's difficult for members to serve their country. There is division in our homes, in our schools, our communities, and our society. Division in our Congress leads to division in our world. The wounds are there and we don't have the capacity to heal them. We are not really practicing democracy. We do not really listen to each other. We do not know how to combine our insight to arrive at the best decisions for the country. Congress as a community has to come home to itself and be mindful of what is happening within Congress. If Congress takes this fourth step, Congress as a whole can go home to itself and be in a stronger position to help lead the country.

The fifth step is for a representative to take care of the people in his district, the constituents who have voted for him. If a representative has a strong staff, and if he can establish good relationships with people in his district, then he can help them to go back to themselves as well. Good communication between a representative and his constituents is critical. If the people understand what their representative is doing and trust his motivations, they will vote for him and he does not have to worry day and night about getting reelected.

Many of us experience social injustice, poverty, and discrimination. We rely on our Congress members to fight for us to improve the situation. We may believe that we can only be happy when the government gives us more or better jobs, schools, or hospitals. But the solution is not as simple as that. There are many other things that contribute to our unhappiness that we may not even be aware of. When parents can't speak to each other, when there is no communication between parents and their children, we suffer enormously every day. The level of violence in the family, in schools, and throughout society is one of the greatest causes of our suffering. We have to go home to ourselves as a country and learn how to practice. We cannot wait for the government to act. There is a lot we can do to improve our situation, even before the government intervenes. A Congress member can inspire her constituents to go back to themselves and have more confidence in themselves. Everything relies on our capacity to practice deep listening and loving speech.

ORGANIZING NONVIOLENCE RETREATS

I urge every public figure to look deeply for a way to decrease the dangerous level of violence in our schools and families. I suggest that they expand current violence reduction efforts to include workshops or retreats that could be organized to teach parents how to communicate compassionately, with deep listening and gentle speech, to remove wrong perceptions, and restore happiness. Teachers could also have the chance to go to a weeklong workshop or retreat every year to learn the art of healing and transformation.

We spend billions of dollars trying to cope with violence outside the country, yet violence within our own country is overwhelming, and we haven't done enough to help decrease it. We have to find a practice that can deal with the roots of violence. Relying only on police officers to keep the peace is too naive. They can sometimes stop violence on the surface, but the roots of violence remain, always ready to explode. Nonviolence retreats and workshops can help parents and teachers bring peace and reconciliation into the family and school. There are those of us with a solid practice and experience who are ready to help, and we don't need money to do it. We only need those skilled in mindfulness and reconciliation to come together and begin to make the plans on a national level.

These suggestions are the basic practice of peace. Peace means the absence of violence, first in our families, then in our schools, then in our society. There are concrete things we can do to bring about healing, transformation, and reconciliation. During a retreat, you receive daily teachings as a kind of spiritual rain that waters the seeds of understanding and compassion in you. On the fourth day of the retreat, the seed of compassion in you is strong, and you are then capable of listening deeply and using loving speech to restore communication with those you love. On the fifth day, we urge people to contact their beloved ones and practice reconciliation before the end of the retreat. Wherever we offer retreats, in whatever language, miracles of reconciliation and healing happen. Because their seeds of compassion, understanding, and awakening have been watered, people are capable of listening to each other and seeing their co-responsibility for any conflict or suffering.

Congress could initiate legislation that would give parents and schoolteachers paid leave to attend a workshop or retreat of mindfulness every year. This one week retreat would help them to heal and reconcile with themselves and their families so that they could become better parents and teachers. Congress could support a practice of peace and reconciliation characterized by compassion and nonviolence.

Our spiritual and religious leaders could help realize this kind of peace action. Part of their job is to bring a spiritual dimension to our social-political life, but it is important to organize mindfulness retreats in a nonsectarian way. You don't have to be Buddhist, have a Buddha statue, burn incense, or bow, to practice reconciliation and healing. In 2003, our community organized a nonsectarian retreat for police officers and criminal justice workers in Madison, Wisconsin. Before the retreat started, we received many letters protesting a Buddhist retreat for police officers. Some people felt it was a violation of the separation of church and state. Those in the Madison police department answered clearly that the retreat would not be religious. And in fact, we only practiced to walk, sit, eat, listen, and speak in mindfulness. We didn't worship; we didn't do anything religious. Yet the atmosphere was very spiritual.

At that retreat, I offered a nonsectarian version of the Three Refuges, the traditional Buddhist affirmation. I offer this version to you here.

I have confidence in the capacity of all beings to attain great understanding, peace, and love.

I have confidence in the practice, which helps us to walk on the path of great understanding, peace, and love.

I have confidence in the community, which is committed to the practice of understanding, peace, and love.

I also offer the Five Mindfulness Trainings, which are a concrete expression of the practice of mindfulness, and are already expressed in nonsectarian language. Practicing Christians, Jews, Muslims, and people of other faiths have formally received these trainings and rely on them as a support for living a mindful, compassionate life.

The First Mindfulness Training

Aware of the suffering caused by the destruction of life, I am committed to cultivating compassion and learning ways to protect the lives of people, animals, plants, and minerals. I am determined not to kill, not to let others kill, and not to support any act of killing in the world, in my thinking, and in my way of life.

The Second Mindfulness Training

Aware of the suffering caused by exploitation, social injustice, stealing, and oppression, I am committed to cultivating loving kindness and learning ways to work for the well-being of people, animals, plants, and minerals. I will practice generosity by sharing my time, energy, and material resources with those who are in real need. I am determined not to steal and not to possess anything that should belong to others. I will respect the property of others, but I will prevent others from profiting from human suffering or the suffering of other species on Earth.

The Third Mindfulness Training

Aware of the suffering caused by sexual misconduct, I am committed to cultivating responsibility and learning ways to protect the safety and integrity of individuals, couples, families, and society. I am determined not to engage in sexual relations without love and a long-term commitment. To preserve the happiness of myself and others, I am determined to respect my commitments and the commitments of others. I will do everything in my power to protect children from sexual abuse and to prevent couples and families from being broken by sexual misconduct.

The Fourth Mindfulness Training

Aware of the suffering caused by unmindful speech and the inability to listen to others, I am committed to cultivating loving speech and deep listening in order to bring joy and happiness to others and relieve others of their suffering. Knowing that words can create happiness or suffering, I am determined to speak truthfully, with words that inspire self-confidence, joy, and hope. I will not spread news that I do not know to be certain and will not criticize or condemn things of which I am not sure. I will refrain from uttering words that can cause division or discord, or that can cause the family or the community to break. I am determined to make all efforts to reconcile and resolve all conflicts, however small.

The Fifth Mindfulness Training

Aware of the suffering caused by unmindful consumption, I am committed to cultivating good health, both physical and mental, for myself, my family, and my society by practicing mindful eating, drinking, and consuming. I will ingest only items that preserve peace, well-being, and joy in my body, in my consciousness, and in the collective body and consciousness of my family and society. I am determined not to use alcohol or any other intoxicant or to ingest foods or other items that contain toxins, such as certain television programs, magazines, books, films, and conversations. I am aware that to damage my body or my consciousness with these poisons is to betray my ancestors, my parents, my society, and future generations. I will work to transform violence, fear, anger, and confusion in myself and in society by practicing a diet for myself and for society. I understand that a proper diet is crucial for self-transformation and for the transformation of society.

The practice of mindfulness can be universal. You don't have to be

Buddhist; you don't have to eat with chopsticks or wear a long robe to be able to practice.

Cultivating Mindfulness

There is much stress, worry, and fear in the life of a congressperson. Their lives are very hard and they are extremely busy. They spend a great deal of their time campaigning to be reelected. Learning to walk mindfully and enjoy every step on Capitol Hill is a big challenge. After the retreat, one congressman told us that now he always practices walking mindfully from his office to the congressional chamber. He can't imagine his day without this practice. The congressional retreat ended with a sharing in a circle and each person had a chance to express him or herself. One Congress member shared, "This is the first time in my life that I have ever eaten mindfully, in silence." Most of them said that they didn't expect the retreat to be so relaxing and nourishing.

One of the Congress people asked me, "What would you recommend as some first, practical steps for people of different races and backgrounds to begin to close the gap of racism and bigotry that we experience right now, and that is expanding now to Arab Americans because of September 11th? Also, how do we deal with the legitimate fears after September 11, 2001 that cause us to look at even our own Arab American citizens in a hostile, distant way? How would you see individuals begin to close the gap?"

I told him that we have to wake up to the fact that everything is connected to everything else. Safety and well-being cannot be individual matters anymore. If the other group is not safe, there is no way that we can be safe. Taking care of their safety is at the same time taking care of our own safety. Taking care of their well-being is taking care of our own well-being. It is the mind of discrimination and separation that is at the foundation of all hate and violence.

My right hand has written all the poems that I have composed. My left hand hasn't written any. But my right hand never thinks, "You, left hand, you are good for nothing!" My right hand does not have any superiority complex at all, so it is very happy. My left hand does not have any inferiority complex either. My two hands have a kind of wisdom called the wisdom of nondiscrimination. One day, I was hammering a nail and my right hand was not very steady, so instead of pounding on the nail it pounded on my finger. My right hand put the hammer down and took care of the left hand in a very tender way, just as it would take care of itself. It did not say: "You, left hand, you have to remember that I have taken good care of you, and you have to pay me back in the future." And my left hand did not say: "You, right hand, have done me a lot of harm, give me that hammer, I want justice!" There was no such thinking.

My two hands know that they are members of one body; they *are* the other. I think that if Israelis and Palestinians know that they are brothers and sisters, that they are like two hands of the same body, they will not try to punish each other anymore. The world community has not helped them to see that. Muslims and Hindus also, if they know that discrimination is at the base of our suffering, they will know how to touch the seed of nondiscrimination in themselves. This kind of awakening, this kind of deep understanding will bring about reconciliation and well-being.

PEACE ACTIONS

It is very important for all of us to have enough time to look deeply into our situation, to realize the insight that violence can't end violence. Only kind, deep listening and loving speech can help restore communication and remove wrong perceptions, the foundation of all hatred, violence, and terrorism. With this insight we can help other people to attain the same kind of insight. Many people in the U.S. are awake to the fact that peace itself is the way to peace. These people have to come together, voice their concern strongly, and offer their collective insight. Every one of us has the duty to help create this collective insight. With this insight, compassion will give us enough strength and courage to find a solution for ourselves and the world.

Every time we breathe in and go home to ourselves, creating internal harmony and joy, we are performing an act of peace. Every time we know how to look at another person and recognize the suffering that has led her to speak or act unskillfully, every time we are able to see that she is the victim of her suffering, our heart of compassion grows. When we can look at the other person with the eyes of understanding and love, we don't suffer and we don't make the other person suffer. These are the actions of peace that can be shared with other people.

In Plum Village, several hundred of us have the opportunity to live together like a family, building brotherhood and sisterhood through everything we do. Although we live simply, we are very happy, because of the amount of understanding and compassion that we can generate. We offer retreats of mindfulness in many countries throughout Europe, Asia, and North and South America. When people have a chance to heal, transform, and to reconcile at these retreats, it nourishes us tremendously.

Unfortunately, our political leaders have not been trained in the practices of mindful breathing and mindful walking. They don't embrace and transform their suffering. They have only been trained in political science. It is very important that we try to bring a spiritual dimension into our life—not vaguely, but in concrete practices. Simply talking about spirituality will not help very much. But if you go to a retreat for five or seven days, you can come home to yourself and every day you will be supported by hundreds of people practicing the same way. We always have experienced practitioners at our retreats. You have a chance to be in touch with people who are experienced in the practice, who can offer their collective energy of mindfulness and concentration to help others recognize and embrace their pain. A teacher, no matter how talented she or he is, cannot provide this kind of atmosphere on his or her own. You need a community of practice where everyone knows how to be peace, how to speak peace, how to think peace, so that practitioners who are beginners are able to profit from the collective insight and the collective energy of the practice.

A Healthy World

Sometimes our sense of fear and insecurity comes from looking at the destruction of the planet around us. People wonder how we can continue to survive when we are destroying our planet. The environment suffers because we consume too much and without mindfulness. We destroy our environment just as we destroy ourselves because of unmindful consumption. Learning to consume less, learning to consume only the things that can bring peace and health into our body and into our consciousness, will help heal the planet as well as our bodies.

Congress could look deeply into the matter of consumption. There is a lot of suffering in people in our society and because they do not know how to handle their suffering, they consume in order to forget. When we are able to touch joy by living with compassion and understanding, we don't need to consume a lot anymore and we don't need to destroy our environment anymore. Consuming in such a way can preserve the compassion and understanding in us. This is very important.

We have a Statue of Liberty on the East Coast of the U.S. But in the name of freedom people have done a lot of damage to our nation and to other people. I think we have to make a Statue of Responsibility on the West Coast in order to attain a balance. Liberty without responsibility is not true liberty. You are not free to destroy. If we forbid the kind of food that can bring toxins into our bodies, we have to also forbid the kind of food that can bring toxins into our individual and collective consciousness. Congress members must look deeply at these things to see where our suffering comes from. Unmindful consumption and production is at the root of our crisis. We are creating violence and craving by the way we consume and produce cultural items. If we continue like this we will never solve our national and global problems. Our practice of mindful consumption and production will determine whether or not we can protect the environment.

It is the individual who can affect change. When I change, I can help produce change in you. As a journalist, teacher, or parent you can help change many people. Individual insights help bring about collective insight. That's the way things go. There's no other way. Because you have the seed of understanding, compassion, and insight in you, whatever I say can water that seed, and the understanding and compassion are yours and not mine. My compassion, my understanding can help your compassion and understanding to manifest. It's not something that you can transfer. If you want the president to have that compassion and understanding, you have to touch the seed of compassion and understanding in him. You cannot transfer your understanding to him. It is the same between a father and son; the wisdom of a father cannot just be given to the son. The father has to help the son to develop his own wisdom.

After various retreats, business people, police officers, and Congress members have expressed concern about maintaining the lightness and compassion they felt during the retreat once they returned to their daily lives. The seeds have been planted in them and we hope that they will continue to grow. But they need help. Community building is our true practice. Without a community, our practice will not be strong enough once we leave a retreat. Our purpose is not only to improve the quality of life for an individual, but also to improve the quality of life of the community. Everything you achieve as an individual will profit your community and your nation. So if a community, or an organization like Congress, applies the same kind of techniques or principles that an individual does, there will be great improvement in the life of that community.

CHAPTER FIVE

A Century of Spirituality

I HAVE HEARD some people predict that the twenty-first century
will be a century of spirituality. Personally, I think it *must* be a
century of spirituality if we are to survive at all. In our society, there
is so much suffering, violence, despair, and confusion. There is so
much fear. How can we survive without spirituality?

THE BLUE SKY

The Kingdom of Heaven is like the blue sky. Sometimes the blue of
the sky reveals itself to us entirely. Sometimes it reveals half of itself,
sometimes just a little bit of blue peeks through, and sometimes
none at all. Storms, clouds, and fog hide the blue sky. The Kingdom
of Heaven can be hidden by a cloud of ignorance or by a tempest of
anger, violence, and fear. But for people who practice mindfulness,
it is possible to be aware that even if it is very foggy, cloudy, or
stormy, the blue sky is always there for us above the clouds.
Remembering this keeps us from sinking into despair.

In this very moment, a number of our Israeli and Palestinian
friends are practicing walking meditation in Israel and Palestine. It
is much easier to practice touching the Kingdom of God with every
step here in Plum Village than it is over there in those territories
occupied by anger, discrimination, and violence. I trust that our

friends over there are practicing well so that they do not sink into despair. Despair is the worst thing that can happen to us. Our friends in the Middle East need to know that we are here, practicing for them. There is always something we can do to help the sky clear up, to help the Kingdom of Heaven reveal itself to us, just a little, so that we will not lose hope entirely.

While preaching in the wilderness of Judea, John the Baptist urged people to repent because "the Kingdom of God is at hand." I understand "to repent" here as "to stop": to stop engaging in acts of violence, craving, and hatred. To repent means to wake up and to be aware that the direction we are going as a society is crazy; it is covering up the blue sky. To repent means to begin anew. We admit our transgressions and we bathe ourselves in the clear waters of the spiritual teachings to love our neighbor as ourself. We commit to let go of our resentment, hatred, and pride. We begin anew; we start over with a fresh mind, a fresh heart determined to do better. After being baptized by John, Jesus taught the same thing. And this teaching goes perfectly well with the teaching of Buddhism. Here is the Pure Land, the Pure Land is here. The Pure Land is in our heart. The Pure Land is at hand.

If we know how to begin anew, if we know how to transform our despair, violence, and fear, the Pure Land will reveal itself to us and to those around us. The Pure Land does not belong to the future. The Pure Land belongs to the here and now. In Plum Village we have a very strong expression: "The Pure Land is now or never." Everything we are looking for we can find in the present moment, including the Pure Land, the Kingdom of God, and our Buddha nature. It is possible for us to touch the Kingdom of God with our eyes, our feet, our arms, and our mind. When you are mindful, you are concentrated. When your mind and body become one, you need only make one step and there you are in the Kingdom of Heaven. When you are mindful, when you are free, anything you touch, whether it is the oak leaves or the snow, is in the Kingdom of Heaven. Everything you hear, the sound of the birds or the whistling wind, all belong to the Kingdom of Heaven.

The basic condition for touching the Kingdom of God is freedom from fear, despair, anger, and craving. Mindfulness practice allows us to recognize the presence of the cloud, the fog, and the storms. But we can also recognize the blue sky behind it all. We have enough intelligence, courage, and stability to help the blue sky reveal itself again.

People ask me, "What can I do to help the Kingdom of Heaven reveal itself?" This is a very practical question. It is the same as asking, "What can I do to reduce the level of violence and fear that is overwhelming our society?" This is a question that many of us have asked. When you make a step with stability, solidity, and freedom, you help clear the sky of despair. When hundreds of people walk mindfully together, producing the energy of solidity, stability, freedom, and joy, we are helping our society. When we know how to look at another person with compassionate eyes, when we know how to smile at him with that spirit of understanding, we are helping the Kingdom of Heaven to reveal itself. When we breathe in and out mindfully, we are helping the Pure Land to reveal itself. In our daily lives, every single moment we can do something to help the Kingdom of God reveal itself. Don't allow yourself to be overwhelmed by despair. We can make use of every minute and every hour of our daily life.

GO AS A RIVER

When we act as a community of practitioners, infused with the energy of mindfulness and compassion, we are powerful. When we are part of a spiritual community, we have a lot of joy and we can better resist the temptation to be overwhelmed by despair. Despair is a great temptation in our century. Alone, we are vulnerable. If we try to go to the ocean as a single drop of water, we will evaporate before we even arrive. But if we go as a river, if we go as a community, we are sure to arrive at the ocean. With a community to walk with us, support us, and always remind us of the blue sky, we'll never lose our faith. As a political or business leader, a social worker, teacher, or parent, you need to be reminded that the blue sky is still there for you. We all need a community, a Sangha to prevent us from sinking in the swamp of despair.

Community building is the most important action of our century. How can the twenty-first century be a century of spirituality if we do not take up the work of building and strengthening spiritual communities? As individuals, we have suffered tremendously. Individualism is predominating, families are breaking down, and society has become deeply divided as a result. For the twenty-first century to be a century of spirituality, we must be guided by the spirit of togetherness. We should learn to do things together, to share our ideas and the deep aspiration in our hearts. We have to learn to see the Sangha, our community, as our own body. We need each other in order to practice solidity, freedom, and compassion so that we can remind people that there is always hope.

BUILDING SAFETY THROUGH COMMUNICATION

If we want to be safe, we have to build safety. What do we build it with? We can't use fortresses, bombs, or airplanes. The United States of America has a very powerful military and the most advanced weapons in the world, but the American people don't feel safe; they feel very afraid and vulnerable. There must be some other kind of practice to take refuge in so that we can really feel safe. We have to learn to build safety with our in-breath and our out-breath. We have to learn to build safety with our steps, with our way of acting and reacting, with our words and our efforts to build communication.

You can't feel safe if you're not in good communication with the people you live with or see regularly. You can't feel safe if those around you don't look at you with sympathy and compassion. In the way you speak, sit, and walk, you can show the other person that she is safe in your presence, because you are coming to her in peace. In this way, you build confidence. Your peace and compassion help the other person feel very safe. This allows her to react to you with compassion and understanding, and you, too, will feel safer. Safety is not an individual matter. Helping the other person feel safe guarantees your safety.

Your country can't be safe if you don't do anything to help other countries feel safe as well. If the United States wants safety, it has to take care of the safety of other nations also. If Great Britain wants safety, it has to think of the safety of other groups of people. Any of us could be victims of violence and terrorism. No country is invulnerable. It's so clear that violence and weapons can't guarantee us real safety. Maybe the first thing we have to do is to say, "Dear friend, I am aware that you want to live in safety. I, too, want to live in safety, so why don't we work together?" This is a very simple thing for us to do—but we don't do it.

Communication is the practice. We live in a time when there are so many sophisticated means for communication: email, telephone, fax, yet it is very difficult for individuals, groups, and nations to communicate with each other. We feel we can't use our words to speak and so we use bombs to communicate.

When we arrive at the point when we can't communicate with our words and we have to use guns, we have succumbed to despair. We have to learn how to communicate. If we can show a group we are in conflict with that they have nothing to be afraid of, then we can begin to trust each other. In Asian countries, people often greet each other by bowing and joining their palms to form a lotus flower. In the West, when people meet each other, they shake hands. I learned that this tradition comes from medieval times when people were afraid of each other, and every time they met they wanted to show that they had no weapons in their hands.

Now we have to do the same thing. With our actions, we can say, "Dear friend: I have no weapons. See? Touch for yourself. I am not harmful, there are no guns hidden on me." This is the kind of practice that can begin to build trust. With trust and communication, dialogue becomes possible.

While our friends from the Middle East were visiting Plum

Village a few years ago, I asked them whether they would accept an international peacekeeping force in the area to stop the violence. Such a force would help us proceed with negotiations to find peaceful solutions for both the Israelis and the Palestinians. Some of our Israeli and Palestinian friends said they can't trust anyone. They don't trust the United Nations and they wouldn't trust an international peace keeping force because they don't believe either would be neutral. Fear goes together with suspicion. Fear and suspicion are what prevent us from being together as friends, as a community of nations.

Since the so-called War on Terror began, we have spent billions of dollars but we have only created more violence, hate, and fear. We have not succeeded in removing terrorism, neither in its expression nor, most importantly, in the minds of the people. It's time to come home to ourselves and find a better way to bring peace to ourselves and to the world. Only with the practice of deep listening and gentle communication can we help remove wrong perceptions that are at the foundation of anger, hate, and violence. You cannot remove wrong perceptions with a gun. We are all aware that the U.S. is having a difficult time in Iraq. The U.S. is caught in Iraq as it was caught in Vietnam not very long ago. In North Vietnam and Cambodia, the United States tried to search-and-destroy the communists. But the more they bombed, the more communists they created. Finally the U.S. had to withdraw.

The U.S. often has many good intentions. But in it's course of action, it causes tremendous suffering. For example, in the war with Vietnam, the Americans had the intention to save Vietnam from Communism. It was a good intention, but this desire to save us destroyed us. That's why I have said, "Save us from your salvation." Your intention to help us ruined us. The intention to love is not yet love. We must know *how* to love. True love doesn't destroy the object of its love.

I am afraid that the U.S. is doing exactly the same thing in Iraq. The more we strike against terror the more terrorists we create. The U.S. has invested a lot of money, human lives, time, and resources in Iraq. It is very difficult for America to withdraw from Iraq now, even if the government wanted to leave; it's very difficult to get out of the mess. The U.S. believes that there are countries that sponsor terrorism around Iraq. The State Department lists a number of Middle Eastern countries as sponsors of terrorism. If we continue to use the search-and-destroy model, we will end up bringing troops into these countries as well. This is very dangerous. I think the only way for the U.S. to change this situation is to invest in making the United Nations into a real peace organization and transfer power to the UN so that it can take over the problems of Iraq, Afghanistan, and the Middle East. America could allow other nations to participate actively in building the United Nations into a true community of nations with enough authority to do her job. To me this is the only easy and honorable way out of the situation, and doing this would be applauded around the world.

Using violence to suppress violence will not lead to lasting peace. America is powerful enough to wake up to this reality. The U.S. is powerful enough to find a solution through peaceful communication and reconciliation, forsaking violence.

The Family of Nations

How can we make the United Nations into a true family of nations? The United Nations was meant to be a community, a Sangha of nations. But we don't really trust it and we try to make the United Nations into an international instrument to serve our own national interests.

When there is trouble within a nation, the whole global community must come and help. For instance, in Plum Village if one person is sick, we come and help him, because that person is part of our body and we have to take good care of our body. If there is a member of the community who has difficulties, the whole community has to take care of that member. When there is a conflict between two members of our community, it's not only their problem, it's all of ours. In a family, if two brothers are fighting each other and trying to kill each other, other members of the family have to intervene to prevent this fratricide. The United Nations, representing the human family, hasn't done that. In a community, a Sangha, each person trains to see beyond their individual point of view and to look with the eyes of collective wisdom, the Sangha eyes. It is entirely possible to solve problems using our Sangha eyes, for they are always clearer than the eyes of the individual.

The European Union aspires to act as a family, as one body. I'm very inspired that countries have acted on the wisdom of nondiscrimination. They've put aside national interest to a large extent and have understood that the well-being of the whole of Europe is their own well-being. I've heard that countries in Southeast Asia are considering forming a similar union. Now, we could come together on a global level, seeing that all countries' well-being is interconnected and seeing that when we help other countries, we are helping ourselves.

If the United Nations could become a true community, the tensions between various countries could be taken care of by the Sangha of the United Nations. The United Nations' General Assembly could also be a place where people learn to listen to each other as brothers and sisters. We could stop acting in the name of national interest. In a true Sangha, you can't operate on the basis of your ego. You surrender your individual self, that you believe to be separate from everyone else, and use the Sangha eyes as your eyes. You learn to profit from the collective wisdom and insight of the Sangha. It can be much stronger than each country's own individual insight. Speak out to help others in your community, city, and nation. We have to help the United Nations become a true Sangha of nations.

We can't allow things to continue as they are. Every day people die, every day bombs explode. If people don't believe in the United Nations as a true Sangha, it's because it's not functioning that way. Instead, each country wants to use it to their own advantage. And mass violence continues without intervention. If the United Nations can become a real Sangha body and if the Security Council can become a true instrument of peace, we could act quickly and solve many of the problems of violence around the world. Some people say the UN is hopeless, and that we should destroy it and start with something new. But the UN is already there and it is what we have. The UN is our hope.

The Sangha body of the United Nations can tell the governments of Pakistan and India, of Israel and Palestine, of the United States and Iraq, "You are friends, you are family. Please hold hands with each other and serve the Sangha body." This may sound naive, but it is exactly in accord with the ancient wisdom of all our ancestors. Whenever there are conflicts between people in Plum Village, this is what we do and it may take only a few hours. Instead of fighting each other, we become allies to serve the common cause of peace and stability in the world. It is possible for countries to act as siblings instead of enemies. This is Sangha building in the twenty-first century.

If you're a journalist, if you're a writer, if you're a professor, if you're a parent, please speak out. Articulate your deep desire for peace and reconciliation and affirm your commitment to making it happen. Sangha building has to be done at every level—local, national, and international. Sangha is our hope.

Displaying the Light of Wisdom

Whether or not the twenty-first century becomes a century of spirituality depends on our capacity of building community. Without a community, we will become victims of despair. We need each other. We need to congregate, to bring together our wisdom, our insight, and our compassion. The Earth is our true home, a home for all of us. We invite everyone to look deeply into our collective situation. We invite everyone to speak out to spread the message. If we fail in this task of Sangha building, then the suffering of the twenty-first century will be indescribable.

We can bring the spiritual dimension into our daily life, as well as our social, political, and economic life. This is our practice. Jesus had this intention. Buddha had this intention. All of our spiritual ancestors, whether Christian, Jewish, Muslim, Hindu, or Buddhist had this intention. We can display the light of wisdom and come together in order to create hope and to prevent society and the younger generation from sinking in despair.

We can learn to speak out so that the voice of the Buddha, the voice of Jesus, the voice of Mohammed, and all our spiritual ancestors can be heard in this dangerous and pivotal moment in history. We offer this light so that the world will not sink into total darkness. Everyone has the seed of awakening and insight within her heart. Let us help each other touch these seeds in ourselves so that everyone will have the courage to speak out. We must ensure that the way we live our daily lives doesn't create more terrorism in the world. Only a collective awakening can stop this course of self-destruction.

Writings on Terrorism

A PRAYER: THE BEST FLOWERS OF OUR PRACTICE
Public Talk, Berkeley, California, September 13, 2001

Two days after the tragedy of September 11, I offered this talk. Standing together with my community of eighty monks and nuns, we faced an audience of several thousand Americans and offered this prayer for healing and peace:

Let us offer humanity the best flowers and fruits of our practice: lucidity, solidity, brotherhood, understanding, and compassion. Breathing in, we are aware that most of us have not been able to overcome the shock. Breathing out, we are aware that there is a tremendous amount of suffering in our country, a tremendous amount of fear, anger, and hatred. But we know deep in our heart that anger and hatred cannot be extinguished with anger and hatred. Responding to hatred with hatred will only cause hatred to multiply a thousand-fold. Only with compassion can we transform hatred and anger.

In this very moment we invoke all of our spiritual teachers, Buddhas and bodhisattvas to be with us helping us to embrace the suffering of America as a nation, as a country, to embrace the world as a nation, as a country, to embrace humanity as a family, so that we can become lucid and calm, so that we will know exactly what we should do and what we should not do to avoid making the situation worse.

We know that there are those of us who are trying to rescue and to support victims of the destruction and we are grateful to them. There are those who are dying, who are suffering terribly in this very moment. Let us be there for all of them and embrace them tenderly with all our compassion, with our understanding, with our awareness. We know that there are many of us who are trying to see to it that violence will not happen again. We know that responding to hatred and violence with compassion is the only path for all of us.

I urge that in these days when we have not yet been able to overcome the tremendous shock, we should not do anything, we should not say anything. We should go home to ourselves and practice mindful breathing and mindful walking to allow ourselves to calm down and to allow lucidity to come, so that we can understand the real roots of our suffering and the suffering of the world. Only with that understanding can compassion arise. America can be a great nation if she knows how to act with compassion instead of punishment.

We offer this incense to all our spiritual teachers and we ask them to support us in this very difficult moment.

CULTIVATING COMPASSION TO RESPOND TO VIOLENCE
Statement issued by Thich Nhat Hanh in the New York Times,
September 18, 2001

All violence is injustice.

Responding to violence with violence is injustice, not only to the other person but also to oneself. Responding to violence with violence resolves nothing; it only escalates violence, anger, and hatred. It is only with compassion that we can embrace and disintegrate violence. This is true in relationships between individuals as well as in relationships between nations.

Many people in America consider Jesus Christ as their Lord, their spiritual ancestor, and their teacher. We should heed his teachings especially during critical times like this. Jesus never encourages us to respond to acts of violence with violence. His teaching is, instead, to use compassion to deal with violence. The teachings of Judaism go very much in the same direction.

Spiritual leaders of this country are invited to raise their voices, to bring about the awareness of this teaching to the American nation and people. What needs to be done right now is to recognize the suffering, to embrace it and to understand it. We need calmness and lucidity so that we can listen deeply to and understand our own suffering, the suffering of the nation, and the suffering of others. By understanding the nature and the causes of the suffering, we will then know the right path to follow.

The violence and hatred we presently face has been created by misunderstanding, injustice, discrimination, and despair. We are all co-responsible for the making of violence and despair in the world by our way of living, of consuming, and of handling the problems of the world. Understanding why this violence has been created, we will then know what to do and what not to do in order to decrease the level of violence in ourselves and in the world, to create and foster understanding, reconciliation, and forgiveness.

I have the conviction that America possesses enough wisdom and courage to perform an act of forgiveness and compassion, and I know that such an act can bring great relief to America and to the world right away.

WHAT I WOULD SAY TO OSAMA BIN LADEN
beliefnet.com Interview, September 2001

beliefnet: If you could speak to Osama bin Laden, what would you say to him? Likewise, if you were to speak to the American people, what would you suggest we do at this point, individually and as a nation?

Thich Nhat Hanh: If I were given the opportunity to be face to face with Osama bin Laden, the first thing I would do is listen. I would try to understand why he had acted in that cruel way. I would try to understand all of the suffering that had led him to violence. It might not be easy to listen in that way, so I would have to remain calm and lucid. I would need several friends with me, who are strong in the practice of deep listening, listening without reacting, without judging and blaming. In this way, an atmosphere of support would be created for this person and those connected so that they could share completely and trust that they are really being heard.

After listening for some time, we might need to take a break to allow what has been said to enter into our consciousness. Only when we felt calm and lucid would we respond. We would respond point by point to what had been said. We would respond gently but firmly in such a way as to help them discover their own misunderstandings so that of their own will they will stop committing violent acts.

For the American people, I would suggest that we do everything we can to restore our calm and our lucidity before responding to the situation. To respond too quickly before we have much understanding of the situation may be very dangerous. The first thing we can do is to cool the flames of anger and hatred that are so strong in us. As mentioned before, it is crucial to look at the way we feed the hatred and violence within us and to take immediate steps to cut off the nourishment for our hatred and violence.

When we react out of fear and hatred, we do not yet have a deep understanding of the situation. Our action will only be a very quick and superficial way of responding to the situation and not much true benefit and healing will occur. Yet if we wait and follow the process of calming our anger, looking deeply into the situation, and listening with great will to understand the roots of suffering that are the cause of the violent actions, only then will we have sufficient insight to respond in such a way that healing and reconciliation can be realized for everyone involved.

In South Africa, the Truth and Reconciliation Commission has made attempts to realize this. All the parties involved in violence and injustice agreed to listen to each other in a calm and supportive environment, to look together deeply at the roots of violent acts and to find some way of making peace. The presence of strong spiritual leaders is very helpful to support and maintain such an environment. We can look at this model for resolving conflicts that are arising right in the present moment; we do not have to wait many years to realize this.

beliefnet: You personally experienced the devastation caused by the war fought in Vietnam and you worked to end the hostilities there. What do you say to people who are grief-stricken and enraged because they have lost loved ones in the terrorist attack?

TNH: I did lose my spiritual sons and daughters during the Vietnam war when they entered the fighting zone trying to save those under the bombs. Some were murdered because of a misunderstanding that they were supporting the other side. When I looked at the slain corpses of my spiritual children, I suffered deeply.

I understand the suffering of those who have lost beloved ones in this tragedy. In situations of great loss and grief, I had to find my calm in order to restore my lucidity and my heart of understanding and compassion. With the practice of deep looking, I realized that if we respond to cruelty with cruelty, injustice and suffering will only increase.

When the village of Ben Tre village in Vietnam was bombed and 300,000 homes were destroyed, the pilots told journalists that they had destroyed the village in order to save it. I was shocked and angry when I heard this. I practiced walking calmly and gently on the earth to bring back my calm mind and peaceful heart.

Although it was very challenging to maintain my openness in such moments, it was crucial not to respond in any way until I had calmness and clarity about the situation. To respond with violence and hatred would only damage myself and those around me. All of us practiced looking deeply into the suffering of the people inflicting violence on us, to understand them more deeply and to understand ourselves more deeply. With this understanding, we were able to produce compassion and to relieve our own suffering and that of the other side.

beliefnet: What is the "right action" to take with regard to responding to terrorist attacks? Should we seek justice through military action? Through judicial processes? Is military action and/or retaliation justified if it can prevent future innocents from being killed?

TNH: All violence is injustice. The fire of hatred and violence cannot be extinguished by adding more hatred and violence to the fire. The only antidote to violence is compassion. And what is compassion made of? It is made of understanding. When there is no understanding, how can we feel compassion, how can we begin to relieve the great suffering that is there? So understanding is the very real foundation upon which we build our compassion.

How do we gain the understanding and insight to guide us through such incredibly challenging moments that we now face in America? To understand, we must find paths of communication so that we can listen to those who desperately are calling out for our understanding—because such an act of violence is a desperate call for attention and for help.

How can we listen in a calm and clear way so that we don't immediately kill the chance for understanding to develop? As a nation we need to look into this: how to create the situations for deep listening to occur so that our response to the situation may arise out of our calm and clear mind. Clarity is a great offering that we can make at this time.

There are people who want one thing only: revenge. In the Buddhist scriptures, the Buddha said that by using hatred to answer hatred, there would only be an escalation of hatred. But if we use compassion to embrace those who have harmed us, it will greatly defuse the bomb in our hearts and in theirs.

So how can we bring about a drop of compassion that can put out the fire of hatred? You know, they do not sell compassion in the supermarket. If they sold compassion, we would only need to bring it home and we could solve the problem of hatred and violence in the world very easily. But compassion can only be produced in our own heart by our own practice.

America is burning with hatred. We have to tell our friends, "You are children of Christ, of Mohammed, of Moses, and of the Buddha." You have to return to yourselves and look deeply and find out why this violence happened. Why is there so much hatred? What lies under all this violence? Why do they hate so much that they would sacrifice their own lives and bring about so much suffering to other people? Why would these young people, full of vitality and strength, have chosen to lose their lives, to commit such violence? That is what we have to understand.

We have to find a way to stop violence, of course. If need be, we have to put the men responsible in prison. But the important thing is to look deeply and ask, "Why did that happen? What responsibility do we have in that happening?" Maybe they misunderstood us. But what has made them misunderstand us so much to make them hate so much?

The method of the Buddha is to look deeply to see the source of suffering; the source of the violence. If we have violence within ourselves, any action can make that violence explode. This energy of hatred and violence can be very great and when we see that in the other person, then we feel sorry for them. When we feel sorry for them, the drop of compassion is born in our hearts and we feel so much happier and so much more at peace in ourselves. That produces the nectar of compassion within ourselves.

If you come to the monastery, it is in order to learn how to look deeply, so that whenever you suffer and feel angry, the drop of compassion in your heart can come out and can put out the fever of anger. Only the drop of compassion can put out the flames of hatred.

We must look deeply and honestly at our present situation. If we are able to see the sources for the suffering within ourselves and within the other person, we can begin to unravel the cycle of hatred and violence. When our house is on fire, we must first put out the fire before investigating its cause. Likewise, if we first extinguish the anger and hatred in our own heart, we will have a chance to deeply investigate the situation with clarity and insight in order to determine all the causes and conditions that have contributed to the hatred and violence we are experiencing within ourselves and within our world.

The "right action" is the action that results in the fires of hatred and violence being extinguished.

beliefnet: Do you believe that evil exists? And, if so, would you consider terrorists to be evil persons?

TNH: Evil exists. God exists also. Evil and God are two sides of ourselves. God is that great understanding, that great love within us.

That is what we call Buddha also, the enlightened mind that is able to see through all ignorance.

What is evil? It is when the face of God, the face of the Buddha within us has become hidden. It is up to us to choose whether the evil side becomes more important, or whether the side of God and the Buddha shines out. Although the side of great ignorance, of evil, may be manifesting strongly at one time, that does not mean that God is not there.

It is said clearly in the Bible, "Forgive them, for they know not what they do." This means that an act of evil is an act of great ignorance and misunderstanding. Perhaps many wrong perceptions are behind an act of evil; we have to see that ignorance and misunderstanding are the root of the evil. Every human being contains within him or herself all the elements of great understanding, great compassion, and also ignorance, hatred, and violence.

beliefnet: In your book *Anger*, you give an example of "compassionate listening" as a tool to heal families. Can that tool be used at a national level, and if so, how would that work?

TNH: This past summer a group of Palestinians and Israelis came to Plum Village, the practice center where I live in southern France, to learn and practice the arts of deep listening and loving speech. (Around 1,600 people come to Plum Village each summer from over a dozen countries to listen and to learn how to bring peace and understanding to their daily lives.) The group of Palestinians and Israelis participated in the daily schedule of walking meditation, sitting meditation, and silent meals, and they also received train-ing on how to listen and speak to each other in such a way that more understanding and peace could be possible between them as indi-viduals and as nations.

With the guidance and support of the monks and nuns, they sat down and listened to each other. When one person spoke, no one interrupted him or her. Everyone practiced mindfulness of their breathing and listening in such a way that the other person felt heard and understood.

When a person spoke, they refrained from using words of blame, hatred, and condemnation. They spoke in an atmosphere of trust and respect. From these dialogues the participating Palestini-ans and Israelis realized that both sides suffer from fear. They appreciated the practice of deep listening and made arrangements to share what they had learned with others upon returning to their home countries.

We recommended that the Palestinians and Israelis talk about their suffering, fears, and despair in a public forum that all the world could hear. We could all listen without judging, without condemn-ing in order to understand the experience of both sides. This would prepare the ground of understanding for peace talks to occur.

The same situation now exists between the American people and people of Islamic and Arabic nations. There is much misunder-standing. The lack of communication hinders our ability to resolve our difficulties peacefully.

beliefnet: Compassion is a very large part of Buddhism and Buddhist practice. But at this point in time, compassion towards terrorists seems impossible to muster. Is it realistic to think people can feel true compassion now?

TNH: Without understanding, compassion is impossible. When you understand the suffering of others, you do not have to force yourself to feel compassion, the door of your heart will just naturally open. All of the hijackers were so young and yet they sacrificed their lives for what? Why did they do that? What kind of deep suffering is there? It will require deep listening and deep looking to understand that.

To have compassion in this situation is to perform a great act of forgiveness. We can first embrace the suffering, both outside of America and within America. We need to look after the victims here within our country and also to have compassion for the hijackers and their families because they are also victims of ignorance and hatred. In this way we can truly practice nondiscrimination. We do not need to wait many years or decades to realize reconciliation and forgiveness. We need a wake up call now in order not to allow hatred to overwhelm our hearts.

beliefnet: Do you believe things happen for a reason? If so, what was the reason for the attacks on the United States?

TNH: The deep reason for our current situation is our patterns of consumption. U.S. citizens consume sixty percent of the world's energy resources yet they account for only six percent of the world's total population. Children in America witness 100,000 acts of violence on television by the time they finish elementary school. Another reason for our current situation is our foreign policy and the lack of deep listening within our relationships. We do not use deep listening to understand the suffering and the real needs of people in other nations.

beliefnet: What do you think would be the most effective spiritual response to this tragedy?

TNH: We can begin right now to practice calming our anger, looking deeply at the roots of the hatred and violence in our society and in our world, and listening with compassion in order to hear and understand what we have not yet had the capacity to hear and to understand. When the drop of compassion begins to form in our hearts and minds, we begin to develop concrete responses to our situation. When we have listened and looked deeply, we may begin to develop the energy of brotherhood and sisterhood between all nations, which is the deepest spiritual heritage of all religious and cultural traditions. In this way the peace and understanding within the whole world is increased day by day.

To develop the drop of compassion in our own heart is the only effective spiritual response to hatred and violence. That drop of compassion will be the result of calming our anger, looking deeply at the roots of our own violence, deep listening, and understanding the suffering of everyone involved in the acts of hatred and violence.

Practices for Peace

IN THIS BOOK, I recommend various practices for people wondering how to respond to terrorism and the fear that they live with every day. Below I have listed these key practices, as well as some suggestions on how to practice them in a variety of settings and situations.

WALKING MEDITATION

> The mind can go in a thousand directions.
> But on this beautiful path, I walk in peace.
> With each step, a gentle wind blows.
> With each step, a flower blooms.

Walking meditation is meditation while walking. We walk slowly, in a relaxed way, keeping a light smile on our lips. When we practice this way, we feel deeply at ease, and our steps are those of the most secure person on Earth. Walking meditation is really to enjoy the walking—walking not in order to arrive, just for walking, to be in the present moment, and to enjoy each step. Therefore you have to shake off all worries and anxieties, not thinking of the future, not thinking of the past, just enjoying the present moment. Anyone can do it. It takes only a little time, a little mindfulness, and the wish to be happy.

We walk all the time, but usually it is more like running. Our hurried steps print anxiety and sorrow on the Earth. If we can take one step in peace, we can take two, three, four, and then five steps for the peace and happiness of humankind.

Our mind darts from one thing to another, like a monkey swinging from branch to branch without stopping to rest. Thoughts have millions of pathways, and we are forever pulled along by them into the world of forgetfulness. If we can transform our walking path into a field for meditation, our feet will take every step in full awareness, our breathing will be in harmony with our steps, and our mind will naturally be at ease. Every step we take will reinforce our peace and joy and cause a stream of calm energy to flow through us. Then we can say, "With each step, a gentle wind blows."

While walking, practice conscious breathing by counting steps. Notice each breath and the number of steps you take as you breathe in and as you breathe out. If you take three steps during an in-breath, say, silently, "One, two, three," or "In, in, in," one word with each step. As you breathe out, if you take three steps, say, "Out, out, out," with each step. If you take three steps as you breathe in and four steps as you breathe out, you say, "In, in, in. Out, out, out, out," or "One, two, three. One, two, three, four."

Don't try to control your breathing. Allow your lungs as much time and air as they need, and simply notice how many steps you take as your lungs fill up and how many you take as they empty, mindful of both your breath and your steps. The key is mindfulness.

When you walk uphill or downhill, the number of steps per breath will change. Always follow the needs of your lungs. Do not try to control your breathing or your walking. Just observe them deeply.

When you begin to practice, your exhalation may be longer than your inhalation. You might find that you take three steps during your in-breath and four steps on your out-breath (3-4), or two steps/three steps (2-3). If this is comfortable for you, please enjoy practicing this way. After you have been doing walking meditation for some time, your in-breath and out-breath will probably become equal: 3-3, or 2-2, or 4-4.

If you see something along the way that you want to touch with your mindfulness—the blue sky, the hills, a tree, or a bird—just stop, but while you do, continue breathing mindfully. You can keep the object of your contemplation alive by means of mindful breathing. If you don't breathe consciously, sooner or later your thinking will settle back in, and the bird or the tree will disappear. Always stay with your breathing.

When you walk, you might like to take the hand of a child. She will receive your concentration and stability, and you will receive her freshness and innocence. From time to time, she may want to run ahead and then wait for you to catch up. A child is a bell of mindfulness, reminding us how wonderful life is. At Plum Village, I teach the young people a simple verse to practice while walking: "Yes, yes, yes" as they breathe in, and, "Thanks, thanks, thanks" as they breathe out. I want them to respond to life, to society, and to the Earth in a positive way. They enjoy it very much.

After you have been practicing for a few days, try adding one more step to your exhalation. For example, if your normal breathing is 2-2, without walking any faster, lengthen your exhalation and practice 2-3 for four or five times. Then go back to 2-2. In normal breathing, we never expel all the air from our lungs. There is always some left. By adding another step to your exhalation, you will push out more of this stale air. Don't overdo it. Four or five times are enough. More can make you tired. After breathing this way four or five times, let your breath return to normal. Then, five or ten minutes later, you can repeat the process. Remember to add a step to the exhalation, not the inhalation.

After practicing for a few more days, your lungs might say to you, "If we could do 3-3 instead of 2-3, that would be wonderful." If the message is clear, try it, but even then, only do it four or five times. Then go back to 2-2. In five or ten minutes, begin 2-3, and then do 3-3 again. After several months, your lungs will be healthier and your blood will circulate better. Your way of breathing will have been transformed.

When we practice walking meditation, we arrive in each moment. When we enter the present moment deeply, our regrets and sorrows disappear, and we discover life with all its wonders. Breathing in, we say to ourselves, "I have arrived." Breathing out, we say, "I am home." When we do this, we overcome dispersion and dwell peacefully in the present moment, which is the only moment for us to be alive.

You can also practice walking meditation using the lines of a poem. In Zen Buddhism, poetry and practice always go together.

> I have arrived.
> I am home
> in the here,

in the now.
I am solid.
I am free.
In the ultimate
I dwell.

As you walk, be fully aware of your foot, the ground, and the connection between them, which is your conscious breathing. People say that walking on water is a miracle, but to me, walking peacefully on the Earth is the real miracle. The Earth is a miracle. Each step is a miracle. Taking steps on our beautiful planet can bring real happiness.

DEEP LISTENING AND LOVING SPEECH

In many American universities, there is a course called Communication Skills. I am not certain what they teach, but I hope it includes the art of deep listening and loving speech. These should be practiced every day if you want to develop true communication skills. There is a saying in Vietnamese, "It doesn't cost anything to have loving speech." We only need to choose our words carefully and we can make other people very happy. The way we speak and listen can offer others joy, happiness, self-confidence, hope, trust, and enlightenment.

Many people in our society have lost the capacity of listening and using loving speech. In many families, no one can listen to anyone else. Communication has become impossible. This is the biggest problem of our time. Never in human history have we had so many means of communication: television, radio, telephone, fax, email, the internet—yet we remain islands, with little real communication between family members, individuals in society, or nations. There are so many wars and conflicts. We have to find ways to open the doors of communication again. When we cannot communicate, we get sick, and we suffer and spill our suffering on to other people. We pay psychotherapists to listen to us, but psychotherapists are just human beings who have problems also.

One day in Karma Ling, a meditation center in the French Alps, I told a group of children that they should go to a friend or a parent every time they feel pain within themselves to communicate about it. Children suffer like adults. They also feel lonely, cut off, and helpless. We have to teach them how to communicate when they suffer so much.

Suppose your partner says something unkind to you, and you feel hurt. If you reply right away, you risk making the situation worse. The best practice is to breathe in and out to calm yourself, and when you are calm enough, say, "Darling, what you just said hurt me. I would like to look deeply into it, and I would like you to look deeply into it, also." Then you can make an appointment for Friday evening to look at it together. One person looking at the roots of your suffering is good, two people looking at them is better, and two people looking together is best. I propose Friday evening for two reasons. First, you are still hurt, and if you begin discussing it right away, it may be too risky. You might say things that will make the situation worse. From now until Friday evening, you can practice looking deeply into the nature of your suffering, and the other person can also. While driving, you will also have a chance to look deeply into it. Before Friday night, one or both of you may see the root of the problem and be able to tell the other and apologize. Then on Friday night, you can have a cup of tea together and enjoy each other. If you make an appointment, you will both have time to calm down and look deeply. This is the practice of meditation. Meditation is to calm ourselves and to look deeply into the nature of our suffering.

When Friday night comes, if the suffering has not been transformed, you will be able to practice the art of Avalokiteshvara—one person expressing herself, while the other person listens deeply.[4] When you speak, you tell the deepest kind of truth, using loving speech, the kind of speech the other person can understand and accept. While listening, you know that your listening must be of a good quality to relieve the other person of his suffering. A second reason for waiting until Friday is that when you neutralize that feeling on Friday evening, you have Saturday and Sunday to enjoy being together.

Loving speech is an important aspect of practice. We say only loving things. We say the truth in a loving way, with nonviolence. This can only be done when we are calm. When we are irritated, we may say things that are destructive. So when we feel irritated, we should refrain from saying anything. We can just breathe. If we need to, we can practice walking meditation in the fresh air, looking at the trees, the clouds, the river. Once we have returned to our calmness, our serenity, we are capable again of using the language

4 In Mahayana Buddhist tradition, Avalokiteshvara is the bodhisattva who embodies compassion.

of loving kindness. If, while we are speaking, the feeling of irritation comes up again, we can stop and breathe. This is the practice of mindfulness.

Compassionate listening has one purpose: to help the other person suffer less. You have to nourish the awareness that no matter what the other person says, you will keep calm and continue to listen. You do not judge while listening. You keep your compassion alive. The other person may be unjust, may say inaccurate things, blame, attack, or judge. Yet you maintain your energy of compassion so that your seed of suffering is not touched. Practicing mindful breathing while listening is very helpful. "Breathing in, I know that I am listening in order to make this person suffer less. Breathing out, I remember the person in front of me suffers very much." We have to train ourselves to be able to sit and listen for forty-five minutes or one hour without becoming irritated. Avalokiteshvara is a person who has that capacity and practices the art of deep listening.

We don't want our seeds of suffering to be watered while we are listening. This is why we have to practice. The amount of time we spend practicing mindful walking, breathing, and sitting is important. We have to help ourselves before we can help anyone else. The first time we try compassionate listening, we may realize that our limit is only fifteen minutes. After that point, we may feel too weak to continue. Then we have to say, "Darling, shall we continue later? Now I need to do some walking meditation." We have to renew ourselves before continuing. It is important to know our limit. If we don't know our limit, we will fail in our attempt to help other people.

I have attended meetings where a person, whom no one had listened to, was unable to talk. We had to practice mindful breathing for a long time. We sat attentively, and he tried again and again until finally he could tell us of his pain. Patience is the mark of true love. If you truly love someone, you will be more patient with him or her.

The practice of Avalokiteshvara Bodhisattva is to listen very deeply to every kind of sound, including the sound of pain from within and from without. Listening to the bell, the wind, the water, the insects, and all living beings is part of our practice. When we know how to listen deeply and how to breathe deeply in mindfulness, everything becomes clear and deep.

Beginning Anew

At Plum Village we practice a ceremony of Beginning Anew every week. Everyone sits in a circle with a vase of fresh flowers in the center, and we follow our breathing as we wait for the facilitator to begin. The ceremony has three parts: flower watering, expressing regrets, and expressing hurts and difficulties. This practice can prevent feelings of hurt from building up over the weeks and helps make the situation safe for everyone in the community.

We begin with flower watering. When someone is ready to speak, she joins her palms and the others join their palms to show that she has the right to speak. Then she stands, walks slowly to the flower, takes the vase in her hands, and returns to her seat. When she speaks, her words reflect the freshness and beauty of the flower that is in her hand. During flower watering, each speaker acknowledges the wholesome, wonderful qualities of the others. It is not flattery, we always speak the truth. Everyone has some strong points that can be seen with awareness. No one can interrupt the person holding the flower. She is allowed as much time as she needs, and everyone else practices deep listening. When she has finished speaking, she stands up and slowly returns the vase to the center of the room.

We should not underestimate the first step of flower watering. When we can sincerely recognize the beautiful qualities of other people, it is very difficult to hold onto our feelings of anger and resentment. We will naturally soften and our perspective will become wider and more inclusive of the whole reality. When we are no longer caught in misperceptions, irritation, and judgment, we can easily find the way to reconcile ourselves with others in our community or family. The essence of this practice is to restore love and understanding between members of the community. The form that the practice takes needs to be appropriate to the situation and people involved. It is always helpful to consult with others who have more experience in the practice and have gone through similar difficulties in order to benefit from their experiences.

In the second part of the ceremony, we express regrets for anything we have done to hurt others. It does not take more than one thoughtless phrase to hurt someone. The ceremony of Beginning Anew is an opportunity for us to recall some regret from earlier in the week and undo it. In the third part of the ceremony, we express ways in which others have hurt us. Loving speech is crucial. We want to heal the community, not harm it. We speak frankly, but we do not want to be destructive. Listening meditation is an important part of the practice. When we sit among a circle of friends who are all practicing deep listening, our speech becomes more beautiful and more constructive. We never blame or argue.

In the final part of the ceremony, compassionate listening is crucial. We listen to another's hurts and difficulties with the willingness to relieve the suffering of the other person, not to judge or argue with her. We listen with all our attention. Even if we hear something that is not true, we continue to listen deeply so the other person can express her pain and release the tensions within herself. If we reply to her or correct her, the practice will not bear fruit. We just listen. If we need to tell the other person that her perception was not correct, we can do that a few days later, privately and calmly. Then, at the next Beginning Anew session, she may be the person who rectifies the error and we will not have to say anything. We close the ceremony with a song or by holding hands with everyone in the circle and breathing for a minute. Sometimes we end with hugging meditation.

Sources

The material for this book comes from the following sources:

"The Best Flowers of Our Practice"
Public Talk at Berkeley Community Theater,
Berkeley, California, September 13, 2001

"Cultivating Compassion to Respond
to Violence, A Way of Peace "
Statement issued from the United States,
September 18, 2001

"Embracing Anger"
Public Talk at Riverside Church, New York City,
New York, September 25, 2001

"'Strike against Terror' is a Misleading Expression"
Statement issued from Shanghai, China,
October 19, 2001

"Strike against Terror"
Dharma Talk in Plum Village, France,
November 22, 2001

"Repent, the Kingdom of God Is at Hand"
Dharma Talk in Plum Village, France,
December 24, 2001

"Transforming Violence and Fear"
Public Talk at the Library of Congress, Washington, D.C.,
September 10, 2003

Dharma Talk in Plum Village, France, September 25, 2003

Dharma Talk at Kim Son Monastery, California, September 2001

The Mindfulness Bell, Issue 32

PBS Interview, September 19, 2003

beliefnet.com Interviews, May 25, 2004 and September 2001

Practices for Peace taken from: *Joyfully Together* (Berkeley, CA: Parallax Press 2003); *The Long Road Turns to Joy* (Parallax Press, 1996); *The Path of Emancipation* (Parallax Press, 2000); *Peace Begins Here* (Parallax Press, 2004); *Present Moment, Wonderful Moment* (Parallax Press, 1990); and *Teachings on Love* (Parallax Press, 1998).

Parallax Press, a nonprofit organization, publishes books on engaged Buddhism and the practice of mindfulness by Thich Nhat Hanh and other authors. All of Thich Nhat Hanh's work is available at our online store and in our free catalog. For a copy of the catalog, please contact:

Parallax Press
www.parallax.org
P.O. Box 7355
Berkeley, CA 94707
Tel: 510 525-0101

Individuals, couples, and families are invited to practice the art of mindful living in the tradition of Thich Nhat Hanh at retreat communities in France and the United States. For information, please visit www.plumvillage.org or contact:

Plum Village
13 Martineau
33580 Dieulivol, France
info@plumvillage.org

Green Mountain Dharma Center
P.O. Box 182
Hartland Four Corners, VT 05049
mfmaster@vermontel.net
Tel: 802 436-1103

Deer Park Monastery
2499 Melru Lane
Escondido, CA 92026
deerpark@plumvillage.org
Tel: 760 291-1003

For a worldwide directory of Sanghas practicing in the tradition of Thich Nhat Hanh, please visit www.iamhome.org.